C000201798

Battle of Britain
Britain
D·O·R·S·E·T

RODNEY LEGG

Dorset Publishing Company
at the WINCANTON PRESS
National School, North Street, Wincanton, Somerset BA9 9AT

Frontispiece. The picture that sums up England and Dorset at war
in 1940 — Warmwell Aerodrome and its Spitfires fought the Battle of Britain.

For **Janette and John Paulson**
at the Frampton Arms — the hostelry for
Warmwell's Spitfire pilots

Avro Anson:
flying from Warmwell.

1939

Publishing details
First published 1995. Copyright Rodney Legg © 1995
Published by Dorset Publishing Company at the Wincanton Press, National School, North Street, Wincanton, Somerset BA9 9AT (01-963-325-83) to whom updatings may be sent, addressed to the author. Distribution in Dorset undertaken by Maurice Hann of the Dorset Publishing Company from 36 Langdon Road, Parkstone, Poole, Dorset BH14 9EH (01-202-738-248).

Printing credits
Typeset by Tim Wike and Julie Green. Printed in Somerset by Cedric Chivers Limited, 9a/9b Aldermoor Way, Longwell Green, Bristol BS15 7DA (01-179-352-167).

Restrictions upon copying
All rights reserved. No part of this publication may be reproduced, stored in a retrieval system, or transmitted in any form or by any means, electronic, computerised, mechanical, photocopying, recording or otherwise, without prior permission in writing from the copyright owner.

International standard book number
ISBN 0 948699 43 4

F o r e w o r d

T HE COVER picture tells the story. This Dorset Spitfire was from RAF Warmwell, a grass aerodrome in the Frome valley south-east of Dorchester. It was taken over by Fighter Command on 6 July 1940, in direct response to the Luftwaffe's devastating attacks on Channel shipping and its audacious blitzing of the Royal Navy base at Portland where Affpuddle boy Jack Mantle heroically kept firing his pom-pom at the "Stukas" though literally shot to pieces and dying. He would be posthumously awarded the Royal Navy's first Victoria Cross to be won in territorial waters.

Southampton had received its first enemy bombers on 19 June 1940 and Bournemouth's turn came 12 minutes after midnight on 3 July. The phoney war was over and the Battle of Britain had begun.

The front-cover photograph was taken at Bestwall, in meadows on the east side of Wareham, on 8 August 1940. "UM" were the code letters of 152 (Hyderabad) Squadron, posted down to Warmwell from peaceful Northumberland on 12 July.

I have been able to confirm that it shows Spitfire K9894, which in other accounts is said to have caught fire. In fact it plunged vertically into the ground and buried its nose deep in the soft pasture. It did not burst into flame, which was a flyer's greatest fear. In this case the pilot had not baled out and remained strapped in his seat as the propeller disappeared into the ground.

Miraculously, Sergeant Pilot Denis Norman Robinson was then able to jump down on the grass.

It had been a typical day. Convoy CW9 broke through the German blockade of the English Channel, westwards from the Thames, but with severe losses. Three ships were sunk and one damaged by E–boat attacks off the Isle of Wight and two Royal Navy destroyers were called out from Portsmouth to give help. An air attack by 60 planes was intercepted and driven off but the convoy then fell victim to a second wave of more than 130 aircraft off Bournemouth.

Here three more ships sank and thirteen were damaged. The Germans lost fourteen aircraft. Spitfire K9894 suffered crippling hits in the dog-fights but Sergeant Robinson attempted to take her home, until the fighter plummeted into a dive as he approached Wareham, without giving him a chance to parachute to safety.

Robinson's luck stayed with him. In the next month he claimed three kills – a Messerschmitt Bf109 fighter, a Junkers Ju87 "Stuka", and a Junkers Ju88 bomber.

He was then posted to Upavon, Wiltshire, and went on to become a flying instructor in Canada, until after D–Day. Peacetime saw him move from RAF C–47 Dakota transports to civilian flying, for British Overseas Airways Corporation, next British Caledonian, and finally British Island Airways. He retired in 1978.

Such a happy ending was very much the exception for flying heroes on both sides of the conflict. Here I shall tell the story in diary form, day by day as it unfolded, with coverage also of other aspects of Dorset's gripping war story. For the most part, however, the flyers rise above the background, both literally and figuratively.

It would be an exaggeration to say it was no contest — but in twilight memories the long hot summer of 1940 has become the year of the Spitfire. You may well imagine that you are hearing Merlin engines as you read these pages. It propelled the most romantic weapon of war since Robin Hood and the longbow — which must be a soundly politically incorrect piece of mixed metaphor imagery.

R.L.
at the Frampton Arms
Moreton, Dorchester

January   **Hawks and doves.**

The politicians have split into the hawks and the doves. Viscount Cranborne, South Dorset's MP, cautions Wyke Regis Women's Institute about the threat posed by Hitler and Mussolini: "These dictators have tasted blood and have applied a policy of force and had considerable effect with it. We must make England an impregnable fortress."

Clement Attlee, the leader of the Labour opposition, was a little less specific when he addressed farm workers in the Corn Exchange, Dorchester: "People may ask what I would have done at Munich. Suppose you had a man who was driving a heavy lorry. He drove it mile after mile on the wrong side of the road, and after narrowly missing other vehicles, came to a position where a collision seemed inevitable, swerved and ran over a child. You might ask me what I would have done had I been driving. I would not have driven on the wrong side of the road. The trouble is that the government has been driving on the wrong side. I would remind you that the right side for an Englishman to drive on is the left."

It is not, however, a time when Europe is keeping to the left.

18 February   **Khaki, not hosepipes, for Bournemouth's young men.**

Speaking tonight at a Territorial Army dinner in the Christchurch Drill Hall, Lieutenant-Colonel Arthur Malim, second in command of the 5th and 7th Battalions, the Hampshire Regiment, was unequivocal that "the duty of every young man who is patriotic is to be in the Territorial Army".

He was particularly scathing at a suggestion that the Auxiliary Fire Service had no shortage of recruits because of the attractions of the blue and scarlet uniform:

"We can supply the uniform, not blue with scarlet facings, but His Majesty's khaki. That is where the young men of Bournemouth ought to be — not running around with hosepipes.

"It will be a bad day for Bournemouth and other towns if they cannot get men to take an active part in a battalion of His Majesty's Army, as part of the field force that will defend the lives and liberties of the people when the time comes. Fit young men of the right age ought to be in the Territorial Army — not in those civilian organisations which are all very well for old men who are not fit."

18 March   **Dorchester Evacuation Committee prepared for 4,612.**

A survey of parishes in the Dorchester Rural District, in which Abbotsbury and Maiden Newton are the only significant places that have failed to respond, shows that a total of 4,612 evacuees could be accommodated in the area. Dorchester Evacuation Committee has reservations, however, and will tell the Ministry of Health that water supplies and sanitary facilities are inadequate.

2 June   **Reception Areas prepare for evacuees.**

Billeting Officers met with local government officials for a conference at

Dorchester today to discuss how the Reception Areas would handle their expected influx of children evacuated from London. The local reception centre is Maud Road School in Dorchester, which will provide light refreshments and disperse the youngsters with a bag of food each that is sufficient for forty-eight hours. Quite where to house them aroused deeper discussion.

It was agreed to send 1,600 children into the borough of Dorchester, 1,900 to the surrounding rural district, and 1,300 into the Beaminster area.

2 June   Portland destroyers sail to aid of trapped submariners.

The Portland-based 6th Destroyer Flotilla of Tribal-class vessels, led by HMS *Mohawk*, has been ordered to sail immediately for Liverpool Bay where a new submarine has failed to surface during sea trials. They are to render assistance to the 1,095-ton HMS *Thetis* which has ninety men trapped aboard.

Footnote   Nothing could be done to save them. It was to be the worst peacetime submarine tragedy, with the agony also being extended for days for those on the surface ships, knowing they had no means of helping their comrades who were trapped on the seabed.

Thetis would later be raised. Restored, refitted, and renamed, she became HMS *Thunderbolt* and joined the British Mediterranean Fleet in the autumn of 1940.

June   Anti-aircraft guns issued at Poole.

The 310th Anti-Aircraft Battery, which has 130 recruits training at the Mount Street Drill Hall in Poole, has been issued with the new 3.7-inch AA guns.

June   Territorial gunners reorganised.

The 375th and 376th Queen's Own Dorset Yeomanry Batteries, with recruits from Shaftesbury, Blandford and Sherborne, have been amalgamated. The new Territorial Army unit will retain the historic name, as the 141st (Queen's Own Dorset Yeomanry) Field Regiment, Royal Artillery.

Likewise the 218th Field Battery, based in the Drill Hall at the Lansdowne, Bournemouth, has merged with the Dorchester and Bridport 224th (Dorset) Field Battery to form the 94th (Dorset and Hants) Field Regiment, Royal Artillery.

June   1st Dorsets garrison Malta.

The 1st Battalion of the Dorsetshire Regiment have arrived in the Grand Harbour, Valetta, aboard the troopship *Neuralia* from Bombay. They had been serving in India since 1936. These Regular Army soldiers are to man the south-eastern sector of the island's defences.

9 July   **Dorset tests the Black-out.**

04.00 hours. The lights have gone out all across Dorset and fourteen other southern counties of England. Aeroplanes are overhead to monitor the results. Air Raid Precautions directives state that even a light of one candle-power can be seen from a height of two miles on a clear night.

Urban kerbs, posts and poles are to be painted white to lessen the need for street lighting. The weather has co-operated with this Sunday morning's experiment.

July   **Huge tented camp sprouts across Blandford's downland.**

Race Down, to the east of Blandford, is smothered with more than a hundred marquees and 500 smaller tents concentrated across the former hutted lines around Cuckoo Clump that were used in the Great War to train the Royal Naval Division who landed at Gallipoli in the Dardanelles.

It was here, it is said, that Sub-Lieutenant Rupert Brooke wrote those immortal lines: "If I should die, think only this of me: That there's some corner of a foreign field that is for ever England."

The mobilisation this time is for a Militia Camp to provide volunteers with basic physical and weapons training in a gentler introduction to the military life.

1 August   **5th Dorsets reformed.**

The 5th Battalion of the Dorsetshire Regiment, a Territorial unit many of whose volunteers are from Poole, has been reformed under the command of Colonel Sir John Lees of Post Green, Lytchett Minster. It is part of the 43rd (Wessex) Division. Sir John was wounded twice in the Great War.

Footnote He would serve as an honorary bodyguard to King George VI.

3 August   **'War today...is unlikely' — Defence Minister.**

"War today is not only not inevitable but is unlikely. The Government have good reason for saying that." — Sir Thomas Inskip, the Minister of Defence.

9 August   **The King at Weymouth — It's raining everywhere.'**

Thousands of visitors pack Weymouth to see King George VI visit the town for a review of the Reserve Fleet which is being mobilised in Portland Harbour. A total of 120 ships have gathered. For most in the Royal Navy Volunteer Reserve the last summer of the Thirties has already ended, but on shore the holidaymakers are having their last fling. An estimated 45,000 converged on the station and the situation was worsened by the delay to trains that the royal visit caused. Many fainted in the crush and the St John Ambulance Brigade commandeered the waiting room and parcels office as a field hospital for casualties.

As for the King, he failed to see the ships off Bincleaves because of mist and drizzle. The Mayor expressed regrets about the rain. "Don't worry, Mr Mayor," the King replied, "it's raining everywhere."

11 August   Bournemouth Auxiliary Fire Service in action.

04.00 hours. The second major test of the effectiveness of the black-out has been postponed for twenty-four hours due to continuous rain. Bournemouth's eleven zones of the Auxiliary Fire Service, each with its own local emergency station, are going ahead as planned with their own mass turn-out.

Fifty-four mock incidents have been devised. Five hundred firemen are involved. The exercises are being watched by Home Office Assistant Secretary F.W. Smith and the Inspector of Fire Brigades, Tom Beakes, together with the Mayor of Bournemouth and council officers.

12 August   Radar exercises: 'Eastland' intercepted.

Sustained exercises for the past four days, involving 1,300 aircraft of the Royal Air Force split between "Westland" defenders and "Eastland" attackers, have shown that the country's twenty-five Radio Direction Finding [radar] stations detected almost every attacking formation. This was despite appalling weather, including rain, wind and fog, which caused frequent suspension of both attacking and interception flights.

The taller aerials of the radar stations sent out radio waves from 350-feet, which were then reflected back from the intruding aeroplanes and received on the station's lower set of 250-feet aerials. The fractional difference of time between the transmitted and returned signal was measured on a calibrated cathode-ray tube to indicate the altitude and direction of intruding aircraft whilst they were up to 150 miles offshore.

Air Chief Marshal Sir Hugh Dowding today broadcast on the BBC wireless to tell the nation that the exercise had been successful, though he stopped just short of directly mentioning the art of Radio Direction Finding:

"It only remains for us to see that our technical equipment keeps ahead of that of our potential enemy. What we have been doing is to work at increasing interception towards one hundred per cent which is our goal. I am satisfied with our progress, and I confidently believe that a serious attack on these islands would be brought to a standstill within a short space of time."

Footnote Prophetic words. "Our technical equipment" now included secrets of the German "Enigma" military cipher machines, courtesy Polish cryptanalysts in July.

13 August   Blackout, sirens and Portland mock battle.

Air raid sirens have sounded across south Dorset at 00.15 hours this Sunday and a blackout is being enforced. The lights have gone out on the ships of the Reserve Fleet at anchor in Portland Harbour and there is the drone of air activity. Destroyers are being deployed as "enemy" vessels to test the defences at the entrance to the harbour.

In the villages the death-bells tolled and bewildered country people staggered out of bed to find out what was happening. In Weymouth the news had already got around, or at least among those who had been out on the town, dancing and drinking or laughing with Elsie and Doris Waters. There was a noticeable absence of sailors about last night.

30 August   **Dorchester councillors consider 'war imminent'.**

Dorchester Rural District Council has decided that "in view of the imminent outbreak of war, that the whole power of the council so far as allowed by law, be delegated to an Emergency Committee until further orders".

August   **Imperial Airways becomes B.O.A.C. and moves to Poole.**

The amalgamated Imperial Airways and British Airlines are to be known from next year as the British Overseas Airways Corporation, which will operate under the chairmanship of Lord Reith, the founder of the BBC. Its fleet of Short C-class "Empire" flying-boats is being moved with their support facilities from Hythe on Southampton Water to Poole Harbour.

Here Salterns Pier and its club-rooms have been requisitioned from the Poole Harbour Yacht Club and water runways, "Trots" as they are called, are being marked out by lines of tyres in the Wareham Channel off Hamworthy and the Main Channel between Salterns and Brownsea Island. The yacht club is now the Marine Terminal.

Footnote Airways House was opened in a Poole shop, 4 High Street, and the showrooms at Poole Pottery became the reception area and customs clearance point for incoming passengers. Harbour Heights Hotel was to become the rest centre for those due to embark from Salterns Pier on early morning flights.

August   **Ansons bomb Warmwell 'factory'.**

217 Squadron, flying Avro Ansons that carry the identity letters "MW", is now operational for coast patrols at the aerodrome to the east of Dorchester near Warmwell, where the Royal Air Force set up its School of Air Firing in May 1937. Their last public display as the Warmwell Armament Training Squadron was a bombing exercise for a 10,000-strong crowd at the open day.

Five Ansons came in and a bomb was dropped on a make-believe factory, a building on the other side of the grass airfield, as the attacking planes were buzzed by three Hurricanes. One of the Ansons was "disabled" and forced to land. Forty planes took part in the day, including a squadron of Singapore reconnaissance flying-boats from Southampton Water.

August   **Lyme Bay and Crichel Down Bombing Ranges.**

There will be more practice bombs heard in Dorset as the Air Ministry has announced that sixteen square miles of Lyme Bay, lying six miles off Lyme Regis, will be designated as a bombing range for daylight use. A limit of 120-lb has been imposed on the live bombs that can be dropped. It is to be known as the Lyme Bay Bombing Range.

An inland bombing range is being established on Crichel Down, in the parish of Long Crichel, on the chalky foothills of Cranborne Chase.

Footnote Derequisition of Crichel Down Bombing Range would turn into what can be called another story! Civil servants attempted selling the land to a third party — rather than first offering it back to former owner Commander Toby Marten of Crichel House — thereby precipitating the Crichel Down Scandal [1954]. This caused the resignation of Conservative Agriculture Minister Sir Thomas Dugdale and nearly ended the political career of his Parliamentary Secretary, Peter Carrington, almost before it had started.

August   **Christchurch 'death-rays' excite the newspapers.**

Sensational stories are appearing in the national newspapers that the Air Defence Research and Development Establishment at Somerford, Christchurch, has perfected the "death ray". This is an intensely strong electromagnetic wave which, it is said, can heat up anything in its path — including living tissue — to the point at which it explodes.

Footnote This was no precursor of the laser or star-wars. As long ago as 1935, Skip Wilkins had demonstrated at the Radio Research Establishment, at Slough, that the energy needed for death rays was way beyond present technology. It was, on the other hand, a convenient cover story for the development of radar systems.

August   **Horse-drawn wagons bring out Blandford spoil.**

Contractors with convoys of horse-drawn wagons are removing thousands of tons of earth and chalk from the site of the military encampment that is to be constructed across Race Down to the east of Blandford.

1 September   **The lights go out.**

A full "Blackout" will be enforced from today. All street lighting and illuminated advertisements are being turned off and curtaining must be made light-tight to prevent any seepage through windows. Regulation masks are to be fitted to car headlights and sidelight lenses must also be dimmed with double sheets of paper.

3 September   **Mobilisation as Bournemouth floods.**

The mobilisation of the Armed Forces took place yesterday as the rains fell. In Bournemouth the 750 men and 26 women of the Auxiliary Fire

Service were called-up to their places of duty and found themselves answering fifteen flood calls between 21.45 hours last night and 01.35 today.

Bobby's department store in the Square had to be pumped out, with the loss of two tons of sugar, as did an air-raid shelter. Electrical transformers exploded and the Pier Approach Baths found itself with an embarrassment of water in its basement this Sunday morning.

Ironically it is now regarded as an emergency reservoir for fire-fighting purposes, with 150,000 gallons being held, so this was an exercise which may have to be repeated.

3 September   **War is declared at 11.15.**

This Sunday morning war hums through military communication lines from 10.00 hours as all units are informed that unless Germany pledges to remove her troops from Poland, war is to be declared by Great Britain. At 11.15 the Prime Minister, Neville Chamberlain, broadcasts to the nation on the wireless from the Cabinet Room in Number Ten Downing Street:

"This morning the British Ambassador in Berlin handed the German Government a final Note stating that unless we heard from them by eleven o'clock that they were prepared at once to withdraw their troops from Poland a state of war would exist between us.

"I have to tell you now that no such undertaking has been received, and that consequently this country is at war with Germany.

"You can imagine what a bitter blow it is to me that all my long struggle to win peace has failed . . ."

3 September   **Portland's 'Kelly' finds she is at war.**

Working-up on sea trials off Portland, having sailed from Chatham on 29 August, the newly commissioned flagship K-class destroyer HMS *Kelly* — named for Admiral of the Fleet Sir John Kelly and commanded by the King's cousin Captain Louis Mountbatten — received a signal midway through the morning lecture.

Chief Petty Officer Primrose handed it to Captain Mountbatten. "Thank you," he said, reading it before continuing.

"This is the stage in my lecture at which I usually point out how valuable the automatic station-keeper would be in wartime, when the captain and other officers on the bridge have so many things to do besides keeping the ship in station on the other ships of the flotilla. I usually say, 'Now I have given you the basic principles of operating my gear. If war should at this moment break out, you know enough about it to work it.'

"Well, war has at this moment broken out"

He read the signal: "FROM ADMIRALTY TO ALL CONCERNED HOME AND ABROAD. MOST IMMEDIATE. COMMENCE HOSTILITIES AT ONCE WITH GERMANY."

4 September   **Dorset's first 4,000 evacuees.**

There are already four thousand evacuees in Dorset, mainly children from London, and the number is increasing by every train. Billeting allowances are 8s 6d a head to the host families. Many schools are so overcrowded that shift systems are being introduced, the local children coming for the mornings and evacuees in the afternoon.

5 September   **'Kelly' claims a U-boat in Lyme Bay.**

In today's K Destroyer Flotilla News, the daily newspaper of the 5th Destroyer Flotilla, Bob Knight reports to the crew of HMS *Kelly* on the fishy sequel resulting from anti-submarine depth charges that yesterday claimed a U-boat off Bridport.
    "That's war — that was; but we must not lead ourselves to believe that some of the catch will always appear on the breakfast-table.
    "The presence of mind of Posty in producing a gaff to lift the whales inboard while the ship had stopped to obtain a sample of the oil on the sea in is much to be admired.
    "We all hope that the Kelly's and the *Acheron's* efforts [another destroyer] did away with one of the pests that sank, without warning, the liner *Athenia* on Sunday night [3 September, off Ireland] — and, of course, we hope that the lucky messes in the *Kelly* enjoyed their breakfast.
    "There is plenty of corrobative evidence to show that there were two U-boats here yesterday — one in Weymouth Bay and one in West Bay,
    "The periscope of the former was seen from the signal bridge of the *Resolution* and the M.A.S.B. and the tracks of two torpedoes fired at the *Kelly*. They missed us by thirty or forty yards, so certainly we were lucky. To be missed by one submarine and bag another [later, in Lyme Bay] all in the first day [at sea] is good going."

12 September   **'Kelly' leaves Portland to pick up the ex-King.**

11.00 hours. "One of Britain's fastest and newest destroyers is being sent to France to bring home the Duke and Duchess of Windsor." That's the buzz, following a story in the Daily Mirror on Saturday 9 September, and the crew of HMS *Kelly*, at Portland, have put two and two together.
    Their commander, Captain Louis Mountbatten, was called to the Admiralty last week. Now, they have just been ordered "to raise full steam and make for Le Havre".
    The "Officer X" they are due to meet at the French port is Major Randolph Churchill, son of Winston, the First Lord of the Admiralty. With him are the Duke and Duchess of Windsor, the former King Edward VIII and his wife, who are at this moment being driven half-way across France. They are to be brought back from exile to Farewell Jetty at Portsmouth.

13 September   **Dorchester girls deliver 14,000 gas-masks.**

Volunteers at Dorchester are distributing 14,000 gas-masks and twenty-four men came to the council's depot in Poundbury Road and offered to fill sandbags. By the end of the day they had stacked five thousand.
    The ladies are helping too, particularly the staff and pupils of the Dorset County School for Girls who are cycling the district delivering

gas-masks. Many have been assembled by the inmates of Dorchester Prison.

16 September   **Belgian steamer blown up off Portland.**

The 6,000 ton Belgian passenger liner *Alex van Opstal,* empty and homeward bound to Antwerp from New York, was blown up today by a German mine south of the Shambles, Portland. All forty-nine crew and eight passengers were saved though six have been detained in hospital in Weymouth. They were rescued by a Greek steamer.
    The explosions, heard in Weymouth, are the first to be experienced in Dorset from the current hostilities.

19 September   **'Kelly' joins 'Kingston' at Portland.**

Having attended upon the tragic scene of the torpedoed aircraft-carrier HMS *Courageous* in the South Western Approaches and on 17 September recovered pillows and a lavatory door from the sunken *Accrington Court*, brought up by depth charges, the destroyer HMS *Kelly* has returned to Portland.
    She is joining HMS *Kingston*, the newly arrived second ship of the 5th Destroyer Flotilla, for the latter's working-up trials. Torpedo discharges will be the order of the day.

23 September   **2nd Dorsets on their way to France.**

The 2nd Battalion of the Dorsetshire Regiment today left Aldershot on their way to join the British Expeditionary Force in France.
    The 2nd Dorsets, the 1st Battalion of the Queen's Own Cameron Highlanders, and the 7th Battalion of the Worcestershire Regiment, comprise the 5th Infantry Brigade. It and the 4th and 6th Infantry Brigade make up the 2nd Division, commanded by Major-General H.C. Lloyd, of First Corps, which is under the command of Lieutenant-General M.G.H. Barker. Commander-in-Chief of the Expeditionary Force is General Lord Gort VC.

24 September   **Prayer is the best weapon.**

It is three Sundays on from the declaration of war upon Germany. Adela Curtis, the Christian mystic writer, has told her sisters of the Christian Contemplatives' Community at St Bride's Farm, Burton Bradstock, that she abhors pacifism and regards "the most effective of all weapons in our warfare" as "faithful prayer".

September   **Training for AA duties (without a gun).**

A Royal Artillery anti-aircraft regiment is giving basic training to recruits at Blandford Camp. Very basic training, in fact, as it lacks any operational gun with which to put them through their paces.

1 October   **Hitler's coffee beans impounded at Weymouth.**

In the first four weeks of war a thousand tons of contraband cargo that was intended for Germany has been confiscated, mainly from neutral vessels, and impounded at Weymouth. A total of 513,000 tons had been searched in seventy-four ships that were bound for European ports.

The prize must go to ten bags of fine coffee beans from a Danish vessel. They are labelled: "Adolf Hitler." The little dictator is teetotal.

6 October   **Bournemouth fireman dies in exercise.**

Auxiliary Leading Fireman Reg Cooper slipped from a moving Auxiliary Fire Service van and was killed by its wheels in an accident today outside a disused church in Nortoft Road, Bournemouth. The building is a fire station operated by number 7 Zone of the town's AFS. An exercise was being held.

Bournemouth has eleven such auxiliary fire stations. Eighty emergency fire pumps have now been delivered to the town.

Twenty-five pumps are required to turn-out for a major wartime incident.

7 October   **Dutch freighter sinks off Portland.**

Another ship has been sunk by a German mine off the Shambles lightship, Portland. She was the Dutch steamship *Bynnendyk*, returning to Rotterdam from New York.

The forty-two crew were able to abandon the blazing wreck and watched her gradually sink from the bows, from the rescue vessel that was taking them into Weymouth.

12 October   **More survivors brought into Weymouth.**

The *Alex Andrea*, a Belgian oil tanker, has docked at Weymouth to bring home the crew of a Whitby steamer, the *Sneaton*, that was torpedoed by a German U-boat in the South Western Approaches. She was carrying coal, to the Argentine. A stoker was killed.

The U-boat commander surfaced his boat to watch the men abandoning ship and called to them in English: "So long, boys. Sorry I had to do it, but it was my duty."

14 October   **Dorset sailors die in the 'Royal Oak'.**

A German submarine [U-47] has slipped into the naval anchorage of Scapa Flow in the Orkney Isles and torpedoed the 29,000-ton battleship HMS *Royal Oak*. She turned over and went down into the cold, grey waters with 810 men inside her. The whole country is stunned and there is hardly a town in the land that doesn't have a wife or a mother who is not suffering personal grief.

In Weymouth, Petty Officer William Helmore left a widow in Hillcrest Road with three children, the youngest of whom he had never seen. Seventeen-year-old Billy Savage came from Holton Heath, near Wareham.

Petty Officer Charles Beeling's parents live at Plush, near Piddletrenthide. Twenty-year-old John Hocking had been living with his grandfather at Martinstown. East Dorset's losses include Dennis Brown of Broadstone and Vernon Fay of Branksome Park.

For others, however, the knock on the door that night brought relief after a day of despair. Able Seaman Victor Ayles and Stoker Cecil Lucking, both with Weymouth parents, had survived. So too had Ronald Kenny of Ackerman Road, Dorchester, though the news was not brought to his mother until 2 am the following morning. A call in the early hours of Sunday was also made to St Helen's Road, Broadwey, where police were able to tell Mrs Barrett that she still has a husband, Petty Officer W. Barrett.

Footnote Lieutenant-Commander Günther Prien and his U-boat crew were feted as heroes on their return to Berlin. Prien would write his memoirs before losing his life in the North Atlantic, on 7 March 1941.

October   **Swimming hero distributes Poole's gas-masks.**

Harry Davis, who in his sixty-six years has saved numerous people who were drowning, is taking an active part in Poole's Air Raid Precautions and has made himself responsible for the distribution of 7,500 gas-masks to local residents.

11 November   **The Armistice service takes on a new meaning.**

This Armistice Day is different. Throughout the decade the November services marking the end of the Great War have been expressions of pacifism. They were a communal revulsion at the memory of the carnage in the trenches. Now however they are having a military flavour as the country once more steps back into uniform.

"Once war seems inevitable again, a million martyrs will have died again," Labour Prime Minister Ramsay MacDonald said at the Cenotaph in 1934.

Few will have experienced similar thoughts during this minute's silence. The picture houses concentrate on newsreel coverage for civilian air-raid precautions. The public is being reintroduced to warfare. Joining the armed services had also been out of fashion. Even with high unemployment the level of Army recruitment remained inadequate.

All that has now changed. These days the only partially acceptable pacifists are the "chocolate soldiers" of the Friends Ambulance Unit that has been re-formed by the Quaker Cadbury and Rowntree families.

18 November   **Poole celebrates its silver jubilee.**

Hamworthy Engineering's 300 employees are marking their firm's silver jubilee with a dance at the Woodlands Hall, Parkstone. The Poole-based company was formed at the start of the last war so it does not seem inappropriate to be celebrating the occasion at the beginning of another one.

22 November   **Portland mines claim another ship.**

The German mines floating off the Shambles, to the south-east of Portland, have claimed yet another vessel, the Greek steamship *Elena R.*

22 November   **Five dead but 'Kittiwake' limps into Portland.**

The Royal Navy has also nearly lost a ship to the German minefield in the central English Channel. Five ratings were killed aboard the new K-class destroyer HMS *Kittiwake*, but though listing she has been able to limp back into Portland Harbour.

31 December   **Churchill visits Weymouth, Portland and Minterne Magna.**

Yesterday, Saturday, the First Lord of the Admiralty, Mr Winston Churchill, visited the Contraband Control Centre at Weymouth and went on to Castletown Royal Naval Dockyard at Portland. He called it "my first day off for nearly four months" as he departed to spend the night with Lord and Lady Digby at Minterne House, Minterne Magna. One of their daughters, Pamela, recently married Mr Churchill's son, Randolph.

Today, Sunday, is new year's eve but Mr Churchill will be unable to enjoy it relaxing in the Dorset countryside. He has spent the morning working on dispatches that have followed him from the Admiralty and after lunch he is leaving for London.

31 December   **Year in perspective (and Dorset girl weds a Churchill).**

The song of the year on both sides of the Atlantic is *There'll Always Be an England* by Ross Parker and Hughie Charles: "There'll always be an England/ While there's a country lane/ Wherever there's a cottage small/ Beside a field of grain."

In Germany the Luftwaffe test the world's first turbojet aircraft, Hans von Ohain's Heinkel He178. German physicists split the uranium nucleus with neutron bombardment, causing Albert Einstein to write to President Roosevelt that a "nuclear chain reaction in a large mass of uranium" would "lead to the construction of bombs". Britain and Germany hoard food. The Germans have 8½ million tons of grain in store, with the promise of a million tons from Russia in 1940.

Britain is the largest global buyer of food — taking forty per cent of world trade. Rationing is planned and state intervention extends to the enrichment of bread and margarine with vitamins and trace elements; though only in that is Britain ahead of American food fads.

The Birds Eye label of General Foods introduce precooked frozen foods. Nylon becomes a commercial product. In Connecticut the Warner Lingerie Company introduces cup-sizes for bras. Igor Sikorsky flies the first American helicopter. Al Capone leaves prison, a vegetable from syphilis. German physician F.H. Müller publishes *Tabakmissbrauch und Lungencarcinoma;* the world has been told smoking causes lung cancer. Another Müller, Paul, develops DDT for the Geigy Company and saves the

October 1939. The war wedding. Pamela Digby, from Minterne Magna in Dorset, marries Randolph Churchill — son of Winston — at St John's, Smith Square. The marriage did not last but she did not discard the famous name, eventually becoming Mrs Pamela Digby Churchill Hayward Harriman and the United States Ambassador to Paris.

Swiss potato crop from Colorado beetles. Batman and Robin join the comic strips.

"This is London," Ed Murrow says nightly to most of the 27½ million US families who listen to the radio. His closing line is always the same: "Goodnight and good luck."

Ten per cent of Britons own 88 per cent of the nation's wealth.

The wedding of the year for Dorset's social set came after Mr Churchill had stepped back into Whitehall as First Lord of the Admiralty; his son, Randolph, married the Hon. Pamela Digby, daughter of Lord and Lady Digby of Minterne Magna.

1939—40. Images from six months of war. Neville Chamberlain; black-outs; evacuees; gas-masks; Lord Gort (below, second from right) leading the British Expeditionary Force in France.

1939. Corfe Castle (above) and Bere Regis (below). War games became serious stuff, drawing a Territorial Army unit to Corfe and the 76th Heavy Field Regiment, Royal Artillery, to Bere. In both cases the enemy turned out to be the wet weather.

**1939. Chickerell
Camp. 4th
Battalion
Dorsetshire
Regiment queue
for the
cookhouse.**

**1939. Bovington
Camp. Toast
from the tank
crews.**

**1939. Radipole.
Weymouth boys
carry gas-masks.**

1940. Home front. The Auxiliary Fire Service became desperate for recruits as the 'phoney war' ended and the Luftwaffe took over French airfields.

Opposite—May/June 1940. The British Expeditionary Force, including the 2nd Battalion of the Dorsetshire Regiment, is evacuated from Dunkirk. The figure in the centre foreground, wearing a duffel coat and looking straight at the camera, is Ted Roberts.

17 March 1940. Training flames, for Bournemouth's Air Raid Precautions volunteers as firemen torch a derelict thatched cottage, off Castle Lane.

1940. Portland's Home Guard, in Easton Drill Hall.

1940–44. Bere Regis Air Raid Precautions wardens, in their later uniforms of the Wareham and Purbeck Civil Defence Corps, photographed beside the pavilion on the village recreation ground in North Street. They are (front row) Ken Woolfies, Charles Kellaway, Evelyn Lys, Jock Strang, Gertrude Miller, Fred Lys, Edward Hewitt, (centre row) Frank Applin, Henry Hann, Charles Davis, Jack Legg, Louis Joyce, 'Nobby' Bartlett, Harry Pitfield, (back row) Denis Skinner, Leslie Barnes, Percival Pitfield and Michael Miller.
Kellaway would give the air raid warning on his whistle from an ancient Morris Minor. He used a handbell for the all-clear.

**June 1940. England alone—
the Dorset beaches are now the front line.**

1940 (photographed, after some subsidence, by Colin Graham in 1983). Abbotsbury, across the Chesil Beach beside the West Fleet. Dragon's teeth anti-tank obstacles and a pillbox (seaward, left). The concrete cubes are 3½ feet high and four feet apart, in a double row with nine feet between the parallel lines set on a continuous concrete base.

1940. East Lulworth. Semi-obsolete medium tank from Lulworth Camp, pointing seawards from between the dragon's teeth that block Arish Mell, the gap in the chalk cliffs of Worbarrow Bay.

1940. The invasion coast: barbed wire and soldier at Seatown, with Golden Cap beyond. The 6-inch gun is on Brownsea Island, manned by 347 Battery.

1940. 'SOMEWHERE IN ENGLAND' in this instance is on the meadows at Wareham. Strategic long-distance lines of pillboxes are being coupled with existing linear obstacles such as railways, rivers and canals. The 'Fighting Box' at Christchurch (below) has its defences guarding a viaduct across the River Avon.

1940. Badge of the Coastal Artillery Regiments and Batteries, featuring a muzzle-loading gun and its cannon balls. Not entirely inappropriate — most clifftop fortifications are now receiving their first modern guns.

1940. Opposite and below. Clifftop 9.2 inch anti-ship gun being emplaced and loaded at East Weares, Portland, by 102 Coast Defence Battery of the 522nd (Dorset) Coast Regiment. 'Ever ready,' ran the original captioning. 'Men on duty keep watch as a searchlight sweeps the sea.' The gun then opened fire across the night.

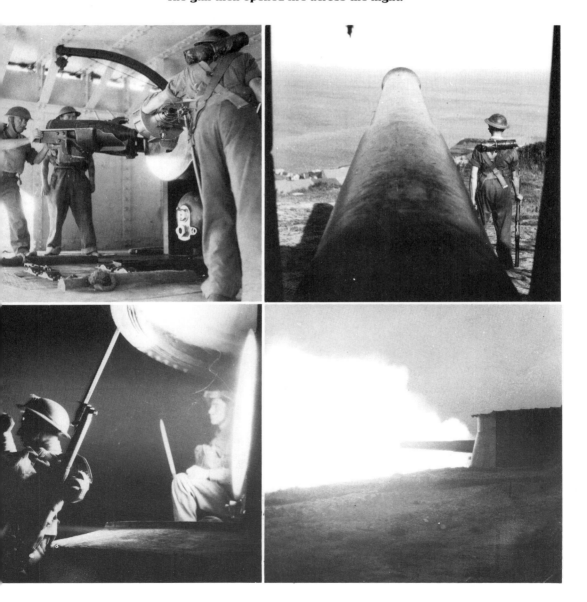

3 July 1940 (left).
Bournemouth's first
air raid was visited
upon Cellars Farm Road,
Southbourne, and the
fire and commotion
caused reports that
German parachutists
had landed.

4 July 1940 (below).
Portland Harbour.
'Stuka' dive-bombers
left a pall of black
smoke rising from
the stricken anti-aircraft
gunship HMS 'Foylebank'.

1939. Portland Harbour. The destroyer HMS 'Brazen' would have a short war—
the Germans sank her in the Channel in July 1940.

4 July 1940. Portland Harbour. Daylight dive-bombers left sixty dead in this wreckage of HMS 'Foylebank', including Leading Seaman Jack Mantle who stuck to his pom-pom, firing at the 'Stukas' as he and the ship were torn apart. He would be posthumously awarded the Victoria Cross: the first the Royal Navy had won from an action inside British territorial waters. A year earlier, 'Foylebank' (below) had been a civilian steamship.

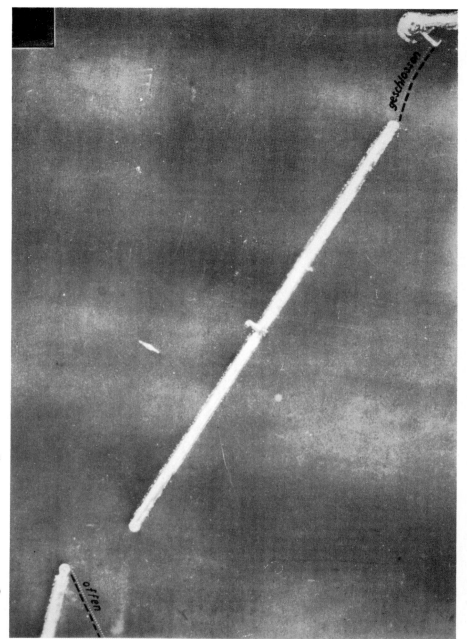

1940. German reconnaissance photograph of 'Netzsperren von Portland'. The central breakwater of Portland Harbour is seen from the north-west. The East Ship Channel (top) is blocked by anti-submarine nets. The North Ship Channel (bottom) is open but also has a line of nets that could be closed.

1940. Portland. Opposite. Luftwaffe photograph of its bombs raining down on the fort guarding the East Ship Channel into Portland Harbour (east is at the top of the picture and north to the left). Note the anti-submarine nets, the floats of which show as a double line of dots extending towards the North Eastern Breakwater. These are the 'geschlossen' [closed] nets of the other German photograph (above, top right).

1940. Wave of Junkers Ju87s, the dive-bombers generally known as 'Stukas' — short for 'Sturzkampfflugzeug'. On 4 July 1940 they sank the 'Foylebank' anti-aircraft gunship in Portland Harbour and on 13 August were back for the Adler Tag ('Eagle Day') attacks on military targets in central southern England. That day's events were a setback for the fearsome reputation they had gained, which pre-dated the Second World War and had been established by cinema newsreels of its preview, the Spanish Civil War.

11 July 1940 (left). First prisoner of the Battle of Britain, Oberleutnant Gerhard Kadow. He was shot down on Povington Heath, Tyneham.

11 July 1940 (below). First of the many — the very first German casualty of the Battle of Britain to be brought down on land. A Messerschmitt Bf-110 of the 9th Staffel of Zerostörergeschwader 76 crash-landed on Povington Heath, in the parish of Tyneham. Seen from the north, in the vicinity of Povington Farm, under British guard. The line of Purbeck Hills is clearly visible in the distance, with Povington Hill (centre) and the slight dip at Lawford Sheard Gate (right) which led to Tyneham Village.

17 July 1940. Below and opposite—Winston Churchill sees the invasion coast at Sandbanks. It is the day after Hitler issued his directive ordering preparations for landings in England.

These photographs sum up the national spirit of resistance, as expressed by Churchill to Parliament on 4 June 1940 in the best war leader's speech this side of Shakespeare: 'We shall defend our island, whatever the cost may be, we shall fight on the beaches, we shall fight on the landing grounds, we shall fight in the fields and in the streets, we shall fight in the hills; we shall never surrender.'

Invasion 1940. Southern Command had its Camouflage School at Poole and practised with the defences at Canford Cliffs. These are at the end of Shore Road (seen before the building of the promenade and cafe).

Issued by the Ministry of Information in co-operation with the War Office *and the Ministry of Home Security*

Beating the INVADER

A MESSAGE FROM THE PRIME MINISTER

IF invasion comes, everyone—young or old, men and women—will be eager to play their part worthily. By far the greater part of the country will not be immediately involved. Even along our coasts, the greater part will remain unaffected. But where the enemy lands, or tries to land, there will be most violent fighting. Not only will there be the battles when the enemy tries to come ashore, but afterwards there will fall upon his lodgments very heavy British counter-attacks, and all the time the lodgments will be under the heaviest attack by British bombers. The fewer civilians or non-combatants in these areas, the better—apart from essential workers who must remain. So if you are advised by the authorities to leave the place where you live, it is your duty to go elsewhere when you are told to leave. When the attack begins, it will be too late to go ; and, unless you receive definite instructions to move, your duty then will be to stay where you are. You will have to get into the safest place you can find, and stay there until the battle is over. For all of you then the order and the duty will be : " STAND FIRM ".

This also applies to people inland if any considerable number of parachutists or air-borne troops are landed in their neighbourhood. Above all, they must not cumber the roads. Like their fellow-countrymen on the coasts, they must " STAND FIRM ". The Home Guard, supported by strong mobile columns wherever the enemy's numbers require it, will immediately come to grips with the invaders, and there is little doubt will soon destroy them.

Throughout the rest of the country where there is no fighting going on and no close cannon fire or rifle fire can be heard, everyone will govern his conduct by the second great order and duty, namely, " CARRY ON ". It may easily be some weeks before the invader has been totally destroyed, that is to say, killed or captured to the last man who has landed on our shores. Meanwhile, all work must be continued to the utmost, and no time lost.

The following notes have been prepared to tell everyone in rather more detail what to do, and they should be carefully studied. Each man and woman should think out a clear plan of personal action in accordance with the general scheme.

Winston S. Churchill

STAND FIRM

I. What do I do if fighting breaks out in my neighbourhood?

Keep indoors or in your shelter until the battle is over. If you can have a trench ready in your garden or field, so much the better. You may want to use it for protection if your house is damaged. But if you are at work, or if you have special orders, carry on as long as possible and only take cover when danger approaches. If you are on your way to work, finish your journey if you can.

If you see an enemy tank, or a few enemy soldiers, do not assume that the enemy are in control of the area. What you have seen may be a party sent on in advance, or stragglers from the main body who can easily be rounded up.

July 1940. Following his visit to the Dorset, the Prime Minister Winston Churchill's warning leaflet — on what to do if the Wehrmacht lands — is being distributed along the front-line coast. It is causing considerable alarm, bringing home as it does the seriousness of the situation, and many of those who have the opportunity to leave are taking extended 'holidays' with friends and relations at a safer distance inland.

CARRY ON

2. What do I do in areas which are some way from the fighting?

Stay in your district and carry on. Go to work whether in shop, field, factory or office. Do your shopping, send your children to school until you are told not to. Do not try to go and live somewhere else. Do not use the roads for any unnecessary journey; they must be left free for troop movements even a long way from the district where actual fighting is taking place.

3. Will certain roads and railways be reserved for the use of the Military, even in areas far from the scene of action?

Yes, certain roads will have to be reserved for important troop movements; but such reservations should be only temporary. As far as possible, bus companies and railways will try to maintain essential public services, though it may be necessary to cut these down. Bicyclists and pedestrians may use the roads for journeys to work, unless instructed not to do so.

ADVICE AND ORDERS

4. Whom shall I ask for advice?

The police and A.R.P. wardens.

5. From whom shall I take orders?

In most cases from the police and A.R.P. wardens. But there may be times when you will have to take orders from the military and the Home Guard in uniform.

6. Is there any means by which I can tell that an order is a true order and not faked?

You will generally know your policeman and your A.R.P. wardens by sight, and can trust them. With a bit of common sense you can tell if a soldier is really British or only pretending to be so. If in doubt ask a policeman, or ask a soldier whom you know personally.

INSTRUCTIONS

7. What does it mean when the church bells are rung?

It is a warning to the local garrison that troops have been seen landing from the air in the neighbourhood of the church in question. Church bells will *not* be rung all over the country as a general warning that invasion has taken place. The ringing of church bells in one place will not be taken up in neighbouring churches.

8. Will instructions be given over the wireless?

Yes; so far as possible. But remember that the enemy can overhear any wireless message, so that the wireless cannot be used for instructions which might give him valuable information.

9. In what other ways will instructions be given?

Through the Press; by loudspeaker vans; and perhaps by leaflets and posters. But remember that genuine Government leaflets will be given to you only by the policeman, your A.R.P. warden or your postman; while genuine posters and instructions will be put up only on Ministry of Information notice boards and official sites, such as police stations, post offices, A.R.P. posts, town halls and schools.

FOOD

10. Should I try to lay in extra food?

No. If you have already laid in a stock of food, keep it for a real emergency; but do not add to it. The Government has made arrangements for food supplies.

NEWS

11. Will normal news services continue?

Yes. Careful plans have been made to enable newspapers and wireless broadcasts to carry on, and in case of need there are emergency measures which will bring you the news. But if there should be some temporary breakdown in news supply, it is very important that you should not listen to rumours nor pass them on, but should wait till real news comes through again. Do not use the telephones or send telegrams if you can possibly avoid it.

MOTOR-CARS

12. Should I put my car, lorry or motor-bicycle out of action?

Yes, when you are told to do so by the police, A.R.P. wardens or military; or when it is obvious that there is an immediate risk of its being seized by the enemy—then disable and hide your bicycle and destroy your maps.

13. How should it be put out of action?

Remove distributor head and leads and either empty the tank or remove the carburettor. If you don't know how to do this, find out now from your nearest garage. In the case of diesel engines remove the injection pump and connection. The parts removed must be hidden well away from the vehicle.

THE ENEMY

14. Should I defend myself against the enemy?

The enemy is not likely to turn aside to attack separate houses. If small parties are going about threatening persons and property in an area not under enemy control and come your way, you have the right of every man and woman to do what you can to protect yourself, your family and your home.

GIVE ALL THE HELP YOU CAN TO OUR TROOPS

Do not tell the enemy anything

Do not give him anything

Do not help him in any way

1940. Poole. School for Junior Leaders with unarmed combat practice in the tennis court of the Sandbanks Hotel (name removed in accordance with Defence Regulations). They used dummies for the finer points of bayonet training in the sand dunes at the back (since built on).

1940. 12th Battalion of the Hampshire Regiment in cliff exercises at Hengistbury Head, Bournemouth.

We could lose the war by Fire! Be ready for FIREBOMB FRITZ!

We could lose the war by fire! *We could. But we WON'T.* We of Britain's Fire Guard will see to that.

Fire Guard work is often dull. Sometimes its dangerous. But it's work that's *got* to be done. So we put into it every ounce of enthusiasm we've got. We watch unceasingly! We train till we're *really* good! We know all the awkward places, and how to get there. We won't be caught off guard as Firebomb Fritz will find.

FIRE GUARD TIPS

No. 3. *Don't be afraid of smoke. A lot of smoke doesn't necessarily mean a big fire. Nor does a lot of heat.*

No. 4. *Don't go into a smoke-filled building alone in case you should be overcome.*

BRITAIN SHALL NOT BURN!

ISSUED BY THE MINISTRY OF HOME SECURITY

1940. Firebomb Fritz. A leaflet from the Ministry of Home Security warns of incendiary bombs. Weighing a kilo, these have a core of aluminium iron oxide, encased in magnesium alloy.

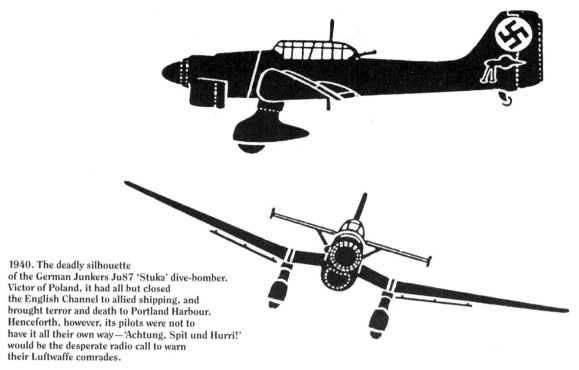

1940. The deadly silhouette
of the German Junkers Ju87 'Stuka' dive-bomber.
Victor of Poland, it had all but closed
the English Channel to allied shipping, and
brought terror and death to Portland Harbour.
Henceforth, however, its pilots were not to
have it all their own way—'Achtung, Spit und Hurri!'
would be the desperate radio call to warn
their Luftwaffe comrades.

1940. Squadron
Leaders of
the Warmwell
Spitfires—George
Darley of 609
Squadron and
Peter Devitt (far
right) of 152
Squadron.

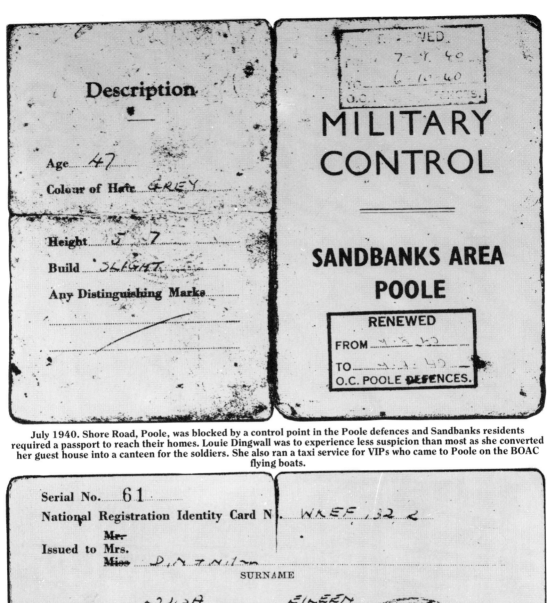

Description

Age 47

Colour of Hair GREY

Height 5 7

Build SLIGHT

Any Distinguishing Marks

MILITARY CONTROL

SANDBANKS AREA POOLE

RENEWED

FROM

TO

O.C. POOLE DEFENCES.

July 1940. Shore Road, Poole, was blocked by a control point in the Poole defences and Sandbanks residents required a passport to reach their homes. Louie Dingwall was to experience less suspicion than most as she converted her guest house into a canteen for the soldiers. She also ran a taxi service for VIPs who came to Poole on the BOAC flying boats.

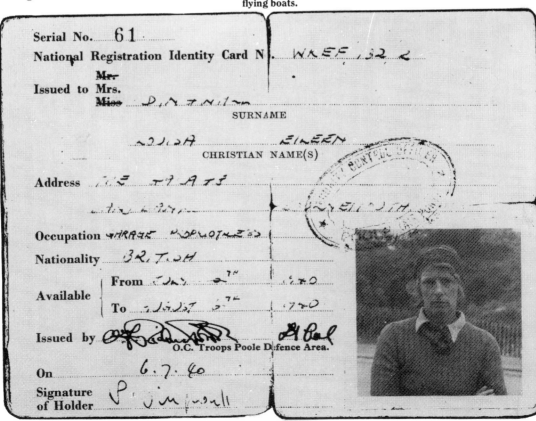

Serial No. 61

National Registration Identity Card N. WKEF 132 2

Issued to ~~Mr.~~ ~~Mrs.~~ Miss   DINGWALL
SURNAME

LOUISA   EILEEN
CHRISTIAN NAME(S)

Address   THE FLATS

Occupation GARAGE PROPRIETOR

Nationality BRITISH

Available From JULY 7TH 1940
To AUGUST 5TH 1940

Issued by   O.C. Troops Poole Defence Area.

On 6.7.40

Signature of Holder   L. Dingwall

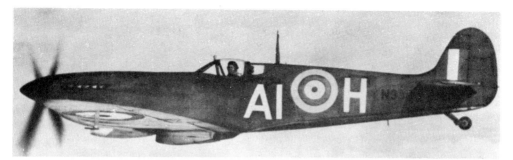

1940. Becoming a legend. There were 187 Supermarine Spitfires in squadron service in Britain when war was declared. A month later 4,000 were on order and are now being delivered. This is a more advanced model, the Mark IX version.

Invasion 1940. Weymouth, on the Nothe promontory. As with everywhere along the Dorset coast, all who could be found guns were pointing them seawards. Regular army soldiers, territorials, reservists and those who declared themselves de-retired joined with the newly enlisted Home Guard and evacuated units of invaded allied forces.

27 July 1940. Naval recognition silhouette of the destroyer HMS 'Delight' which has been sunk by 'Stuka' dive-bombers in the English Channel, south of Portland Bill. Her sinking will show that the Germans are operating coastal radar stations.

8 August 1940. Opposite. Spitfire UM-N — machine K9894 of 152 Squadron from RAF Warmwell — written-off in spectacular style in the Frome meadows at Bestwall, near Wareham. Sergeant Pilot Denis Norman Robinson had no time to bale out as the fighter plunged into the ground. To his eternal surprise he was then able to jump down on to the grass. Robinson had been shot-up in a coastal dog-fight and was trying to coax his damaged aircraft back to Warmwell Aerodrome.

Middle of August 1940. 152 Squadron pilots and groundcrew (back row) at RAF Warmwell, with one of their Spitfires behind.

Front row (left to right):
1. Sergeant Pilot Jack McBean Christie (would be killed in action, 26 September 1940)
2. Pilot Officer Timothy Seddon Wildblood (missing in action, 25 August 1940)
3. The squadron's Adjutant
4. Flying Officer Peter Geoffrey St George O'Brian (survived the war, becoming Group Captain in 1956 and ADC to the Queen in 1958)
5. Flight-Lieutenant Derek Pierre Aumale Boitel-Gill (killed in flying accident, 18 September 1941)
6. Squadron Leader Peter Devitt (survived the war and into the 1990s, having retired as Wing Commander in 1945)
7. Flight-Lieutenant Frederick Mytton Thomas (survived the war, retiring as Wing Commander in 1958)
8. Flying Officer Edward Sydney Hogg (survived the war, leaving as Wing Commander in 1945, and died in 1986)
9. The squadron's Engineer Officer
10. Pilot Officer Graham James Cox (survived the war, being released from the RAF was Squadron Leader, in 1946)
11. Sergeant Pilot Kenneth Christopher Holland (killed in action, 25 September 1940)

Middle row (left to right):
1. Sergeant Pilot Harold John Akroyd (fatally wounded in action 7 October 1940, dying the following day)
2. Sergeant Pilot Edmund Eric Shepperd (killed in flying accident, 18 October 1940)
3. Pilot Officer Richard Malzard Hogg (missing in action, 25 August 1940)
4. The squadron's Intelligence Officer
5. Pilot Officer Ian Norman Bayles (survived the war, being released from the RAF as Wing Commander, 1946)
6. Pilot Officer A. Weston (otherwise untraced)
7. Pilot Officer Walter Beaumont (missing in action, 23 September 1940)
8. Pilot Officer Charles Warren (survived the war, retiring from the RAF as Squadron Leader, 1957)
9. Pilot Officer Eric Simcox Marrs (killed in action, 24 July 1941)
10. Pilot Officer Frederick Henry Holmes (killed in action, 4 December 1944)
11. Sergeant Pilot John Keeth Barker (killed in action, 4 September 1940)
12. Sergeant Pilot Leslie Arthur Edwin Reddington (missing in action, 30 September 1940)

Centre:
Pilot Officer Pooch,
mascot of 152 Squadron,
who was said to have sired
most of the bull-terriers
in the Royal Air Force.

1940. One of ours. A Warmwell Spitfire approaches the Observer Corps post at Poundbury Camp, on the edge of Dorchester.

**Battle of Britain. 1940.
Somewhere in the west Dorset countryside
one hot summer day, with villagers young
and old and at least one dog swarming
over the wreckage of a German fighter.
The scene is in the Frome valley,
photographed by the Observer Corps
unit from Poundbury Camp, Dorchester.**

1940. Spitfire trails in the sky over Dorchester, photographed from the Observer Corps lookout at Poundbury Camp.

August 1940. Flying boat 'Clare' on her return to Poole from the first wartime transatlantic air crossing.

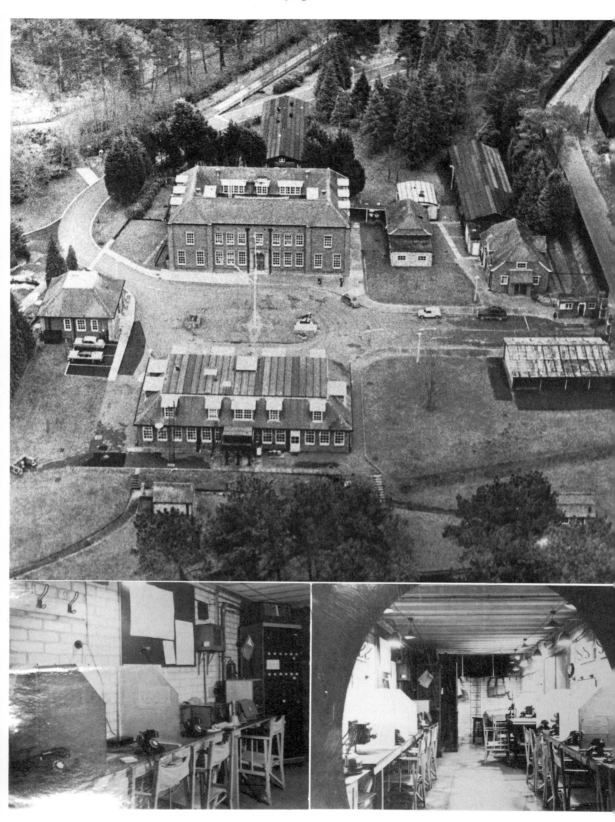

12 August 1940. Luftwaffe air reconnaissance photograph of the Royal Naval Cordite Factory at Holton Heath, beside the main backwater of Poole Harbour. Lytchett Minster village and the Wareham Channel are marked, as is the boundary of the military establishment. Immediately south of it is the Wareham to Poole railway line, with a direct siding from the munitions factory, over the main line, to Rocklea Jetty (right, jutting out immediately north of the main peninsula).

1940. Opposite. Inside OP1 which was the underground control trench for Air Raid Precautions at the most explosive place in the county, the Royal Naval Cordite Factory at Holton Heath, near Wareham. Its peacetime administrative buildings are seen in a post-war aerial photograph.

1940. The Frampton Arms Hotel, proprietor Ronald Draper, across the road from Moreton Station. The closest public house for both RAF Warmwell and its railway station, the Frampton Arms soon became the fighter pilots' regular bar. Seen here in a post-war drawing.

Opposite. 8 December 1940, war artist Cuthbert Orde's drawing is dated. The subject is 19-year-old Pilot Officer Eric 'Boy' Marrs of 152 Squadron, who flew a Spitfire from RAF Warmwell. He would become the station's hero and win the Distinguished Flying Cross — which would save his life by taking him to London for the day, when the Luftwaffe scored a direct hit on his room. But there is a saying about those 'whom the gods love'. In his case it would happen from enemy flak, whilst escorting British bombers to Brest, on 24 July 1941.

15 August 1940. Left. Squadron Leader Terence Lovell-Gregg—killed in his Hurricane at Abbotsbury.

15 August 1940. Below. Pilot Officer Cecil Hight—killed in his Spitfire at Bournemouth. Both fliers came from New Zealand.

Autumn 1940. Four Spitfire pilots of
152 Squadron at RAF Warmwell. Flight-
Lieutenant Derek Boitel-Gill (left)
commands 'A' Flight. Sergeant Pilots
Howard Marsh (bottom left) and Jimmy
Short are seen beside the dispersal
hut, waiting the order to scramble.
Sergeant Pilot 'Johnny' Johnston
(below) is with his Mark I machine.

Mrs. Drew (left) and Mrs. Seaton just escaped death when an enemy plane crashed on their house on Sunday. Engine of the raider is in the foreground of this picture taken in the burned out kitchen.

1940. An engine in the kitchen after 'an enemy plane crashed on their house on Sunday'. The Bournemouth Times does not give the address of Mrs Drew (left) and Mrs Seaton, due to wartime censorship, but the same issued records of the funeral of rescue worker William Henry Vaughan.

12 October 1940. Last evening a direct hit on this unoccupied bungalow at Oakdale, Poole, killed 11-year-old Stanley Ricketts who happened to be walking past, along Kingsbere Road.

1940. Lulworth Castle grounds. Vickers Mark VI light tanks, on manoeuvres with the Armoured Fighting Vehicles School, Lulworth Camp, were key elements of the thin green line which General Sir Alan Brooke, Commander-in-Chief Home Forces, fielded against the threatened German invasion. Some, however, were being handed over, with the 3rd Hussars, to General Sir Archibald Wavell, Commander-in-Chief Middle East. They would arrive in Egypt in September 1940.

August–October 1940. Opposite. 4th Battalion of the Northumberland Fusiliers — veterans of the British Expeditionary Force, Dunkirk and defending Bournemouth beach when invasion threatened — fitted out with motor-cycles and sidecars as a reconnaissance column and training across the rolling downlands of Cranborne Chase.

August–October 1940. From Blandford Camp the 4th Battalion Northumberland Fusiliers rode out into Cranborne Chase, through villages such as Coombe Bissett (above) and manhandled their Nortons across rough terrain.

1940. Portland's submarines slipped away to war, particularly the Mediterranean theatre, as the home-base became inoperable for torpedo training or repairs. Many of the latter are these days carried out at sea, from parent ships such as HMS 'Forth' (left). Cast-iron ingots are seen running in her foundry. Rejoining the silent service is His Majesty's Submarine 'Thunderbolt' (above). She last served as HMS 'Thetis'—until 2 June 1939 when she sank in Liverpool Bay in the worst peacetime submarine tragedy. Ninety men drowned. Restored, refitted and renamed, 'Thunderbolt' is joining the British Mediterranean Fleet. Sir Andrew Cunningham's forces chased the Italian Fleet out of the eastern Mediterranean in July 1940, preventing Mussolini from landing an expeditionary army in Syria.

September 1940. London burning: blitzkrieg at Millwall Docks. Bournemouth firemen are bused to the East End and 609 Squadron from RAF Warmwell is seconded to the air defence of the capital.

1940. German air reconnaissance photograph of the northern part of Portland Harbour. The coastal features (bottom to top) are the Chesil Beach, Small Mouth and the Ferrybridge, Wyke Regis, Bincleaves and the Northern Arm of the Breakwater, the Nothe promontory and Weymouth Harbour. Ships are identified by numbers and anti-aircraft gun sites by letters.

The picture also shows a munitions factory — Whitehead Torpedo Works, on the Weymouth side the Small Mouth opening at the Ferrybridge. It occupies the land nearest the shore, between the road (left bridge) and the railway line (right bridge).

25 September 1940. Westfield Farm, Studland. Heinkel He111 bomber G1+BH crash-landed shortly after noon, having been crippled by RAF fighters as it attempted to escape from the raid on the Bristol Aircraft Factory at Filton. Four members of the crew survived. The white bull on the fuselage is the insignia of I Staffel of Kampfgruppe 55, based at Dreux.

25 September 1940. Wreckage of 'Underwood' and the Branksome Park Heinkel.

1940. Badge of Southern Command, adopted after the Dunkirk evacuation, based upon a representation of the constellation of the Southern Cross. A rectangular version appeared on Dorset's military vehicles.

1 October 1940. Sherborne. Phillips and Son's outfitting department (above, left) and the public bar of the Half Moon Hotel. Below is Foster's Infants School on the east side of Tinney's Lane, Newland.

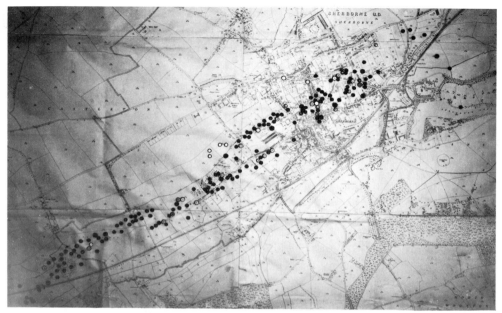

30 September 1940. Pins in the Air Raid Precautions map in Sherborne's operations room, showing the south–west to north–east pattern of bombing across the town. The bombers were flying into the wind. Contemporary claims, reproduced here, were of a total of 300 bombs but subsequent research has shown that this was a considerable exaggeration. The actual figure was about sixty. Counting the pins is of no assistance as the wardens said they ran out of them. For all that, the pictures that follow speak for themselves as to the scale of the devastation.

1 October 1940. Sherborne. 'Homemead' on the west side of Acreman Street.

1 October 1940. Sherborne—the morning after. These were homes on Sherborne Urban District Council's estate in Lenthay Road. The first wave of bombs landed here. Nearby, others dropped in the town cemetery, but not that harmlessly as grief was caused by the uncovering of the recent dead. Eighteen other deaths were to follow from the raid. (These houses would be rebuilt to the same 'design'.)

1 October 1940. Sherborne. Crater and debris in the main commercial corner of the town, at the junction of lower Cheap Street with Half Moon Street. Charles Greenham, butcher, and Joseph Frisby, shoe store, are repairable, but only the props prevent the larger premises of Phillips and Son from following the rest of the building into the street.
(It would be rebuilt in stone to match the surviving corner frontage.)

1 October 1940. Sherborne. 'Stonegarth' (above) was Miss Margaret Billinger's home in Newland, at the south end of The Avenue. 'Sedber' (below, now known as 'Rathgar') is on the east side of The Avenue. Opposite is the centre of Cheap Street, with a crater outside T.E. Gillard's hairdressing salon. 'Have Faith In God' the sign reads above the clearance team.

1 October 1940. Sherborne. Cottages and terraced houses at the Knapp, Acreman Street, left in ruins by yesterday's bombs.

1 October 1940. Sherborne. The German bomb that devastated 'Ashborne' yesterday, in Richmond Road, struck its balcony and ripped off the flat-roofed extension. Its rubble is strewn across the garden (left of the boy). The next-door house, 'Stonecroft' (right), suffered relatively minor damage.
(The houses survive but the flat-roofed extension was never rebuilt.)

1 October 1940. Sherborne. Looking west along Half Moon Street and showing the result of yesterday's bombing.

1 October 1940. Sherborne. 'Tanglin' was semi-detached and is now literally half a house. It stands on the east side of North Road, in the area immediately north of Newland that received a cluster of yesterday's bombs.
(The left half, 'Green Bushes', would be rebuilt to match 'Tanglin'.)

1940. Pilot Officer Noel le C. Agazarian, of 609 Squadron from Warmwell and Middle Wallop. During August and September 1940 he shot down or helped destroy four German aircraft, and damaged another three. He would be posted to the Mediterranean and be killed in North Africa.

1989. Spitfire Mark 1A, R6915, outlived Agazarian and most of her other pilots, continuing to have a good war that was followed by honourable retirement at the Imperial War Museum.

7 October 1940. Weymouth. 'Too low for Double-Deckers' — certainly the case now, with the Southern National bus depot having taken a direct hit from a Junkers Ju88 bomber. Four people have been killed.

9 October 1940. Moreton church, the morning after, in a snapshot taken by E.W. Pride that was confiscated by the military.

September 1940. Sergeant Pilot Edmund Shepperd with Pilot Officer Pooch, mascot of 152 Squadron, at RAF Warmwell. Shepperd, who was born at Binstead in the Isle of Wight in 1917, would be killed on 18 October 1940 when Spitfire R6607 crashed at Tadnoll Mill, between the aerodrome and Winfrith Heath.

6 November 1940. The Heinkel awash at West Bay — see 21 November for the sequel.

7 November 1940.
Pilot Officer
David Moore Crook,
Distinguished Flying Cross,
of Warmwell's
609 Squadron, in a
pencil sketch by
war artist
Captain Cuthbert Orde.

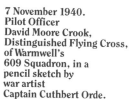

ORDE
9 NOV 1940.

O D.M.CROOK. DFC

609 SQUADRON

Hawker Hurricane:
frequently joined with
the Warmwell Spitfires in
the dog-fights over the Dorset coast.
Hurricane squadrons operated from the sector base
aerodrome, Middle Wallop on the Hampshire Downs, at
nearby Chilbolton, and from Boscombe Down, Wiltshire.
Lyme Bay was shared with St Eval sector Hurricanes from Exeter.

1940. The graceful and reassuring lines of the commonest aircraft in the Dorset skies.
Spitfires from Warmwell had most of their dog-fights along the coast, particularly around
Portland, but they were also a daily sight over the Stour valley and Cranborne Chase as
609 Squadron flew a daily shuttle to and from Middle Wallop, between Stockbridge and
Andover, where they spent the night and were maintained. That practice came to an end on
2 October 1940 and then 609 Squadron and 152 Squadron shared Warmwell Aerodrome as
their home base.

1940. Langton Matravers. Leeson House has been requisitioned by the Air Ministry as an out-station for the scientists of
the Worth Matravers based Telecommunications Research Establishment.

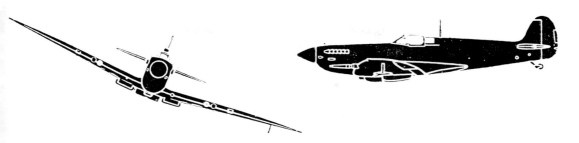

29 November 1940. Where a Spitfire fell: the shattered stump at Field Grove, Durweston Forest. It had a plaque, placed on the tree by Captain Gerald Portman: 'In grateful and respectful memory of Pilot Officer John Frederick Woodward Allen aged 19 years, who gave his life for his country on this spot 29 November 1940.' In 1978 the stump was removed and replaced by a much less evocative granite memorial.

1940-41. Worth Matravers. Air Ministry Telecommunications Research Establishment, Renscombe Farm (left of centre). Seen from the south-west, from a reconnaissance aircraft above the Purbeck cliffs at Emmetts Hill. Four radio aerials can be seen and a variety of radar apparatus. Four separate compounds can be distinguished. 'Site A' is in the near distance on the left, and 'Site E' in the dark patch of the middle distance behind Renscombe Farm. 'Site B' is the large rectangular complex extending from the farmyard to beyond the right-hand edge of the picture. 'Site C' is the small circular-fenced installation crossed by the track in the near distance on the right.

November 1940 arrival, photographed on 17 May 1941. Opposite. Furzebrook, north-west of Corfe Castle. One of the two 12-inch rail-mounted howitzers, which fire shells weighing a third of a ton.

The photographs show the
arming of the shell, moving it
on a trolley, then manhandling
it into a hoist cradle. This
crane arm is part of the
massive gun carriage.

1. Arming.

2. Trolleying.

3. Cradling.

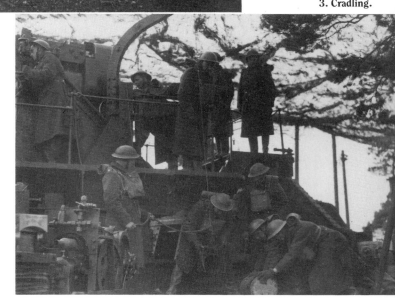

1940-41. Furzebrook, near
Corfe Castle. The full sequence
of loading the twelve-inch
railway mounted howitzer,
carried out by 5th Corps on 26
February 1941 for the benefit
of Mr Malindine, the visiting
photographer sent by
Southern Command. 'One of
Britain's teeth', the captions
would read—omitting that the
fillings tended to fall out.
When used the guns jammed.
Not that it mattered; by that
time Hitler had decided to go to
Moscow.

The top photograph shows the shell, weighing a third of a ton, being hoisted on the loading cradle. This was followed by ramming it into the breech. A shot from behind shows the breech block about to be swung closed. The loaded gun was then elevated.

4. Hoisting.

5. Loading.

6. Elevating.

1940. Lulworth Camp. Sharpening firing procedures at the Gunnery Wing of the Armoured Fighting Vehicles School to the painted backdrop of Dorset pines and telegraph poles in a realistic representation of the road across the nearby heath.

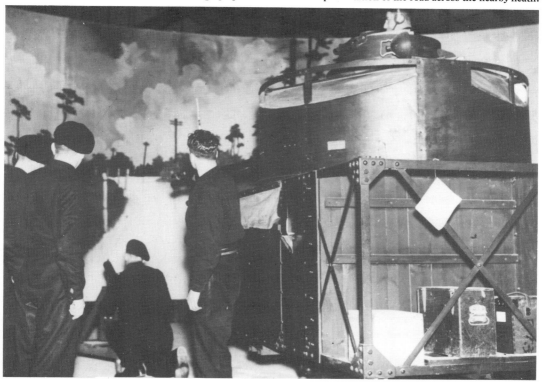

20 December 1940. Opposite. The sea is to burn—VIPs watch the oil slicks emerging from underwater pipes between Old Harry Rocks and Redend Point (top left) at Studland. General Harold Alexander (left) turns towards the camera.

Below—the sands of Studland are ignited in another Project Fougasse experiment. Turn the page.

1944. Warmwell Spitfire etched in wet cement by Bere Regis boy Fred Pitfield.

20 December 1940. Opposite. Project Fougasse. The sea burns off Redend Point (towards the top left) at Studland for the benefit of General Harold Alexander and Major-General Bernard Montgomery—and to remind any German invaders that they will receive a warm welcome.

25 December 1940. Christmas cheer: the Type 15 ground to air mobile radar antenna that was devised at Worth Matravers, built at Christchurch, and installed at Sopley.

1940. 5th Battalion of the Northants Regiment put the Bren gun carrier amongst the turkeys during a little mock warfare around Holdenhurst Farm, on the outskirts of Bournemouth.

1940. The year of retreat and anti-invasion precautions—a tommy-gunner in a cliff exercise at Bournemouth.

1940. Bournemouth. Slit trenches are a normal sight along the invasion coast, though with its protected access and the infantry, this is a scene reminiscent of the Western Front.

**Supermarine Spitfire:
Warmwell pilots fight
the Battle of Britain.**

1940

7 February   **Bournemouth A.R.P. now has 11 Fire Stations.**

Bournemouth's Air Raid Precautions organisation now has its headquarters in the basement of the Town Hall, telephone 7220. All reports of damage of whatever character are to be made to there. The town has been split into eleven zones, each with its own fire station. Some such as the Central Fire Station and Pokesdown Fire Station are regular fire service establishments but most are auxiliary depots set-up in buildings such as the San Remo Towers at Boscombe and Lee Motor Works in Wimborne Road, Winton.

26 February   **Young scientists arrive in Purbeck.**

Several young radio research scientists are being posted to the Isle of Purbeck. Boffins Alan Hodgkin and Bernard Lovell have arrived at Worth Matravers with the advance party from the Air Ministry's Telecommunications Research Establishment at Dundee, which is to set up a new base between Worth Matravers village and Renscombe Farm. They will be joined by Dr Robert Cockburn.
    The group's sole lecturer is Leonard Huxley, who is endeavouring to train RAF personnel to understand and use the complex equipment that is being devised.

    Footnote All four would go on to be knighted in their eminent post-war careers. By 5 May 1940 the whole of the Telecommunications Research Establishment had been evacuated from Dundee to Worth.

2 March   **Luftwaffe attack Channel shipping.**

Long-range aircraft from Kampfgruppe 26 today attacked shipping in the English Channel east of St Alban's Head. The steamship *Domala* was set on fire.

    Footnote Heinkel bomber 1H+AC of Kampfgeschwader 26 — the celebrated Löwen-Geschwader [Lion Wing] – contained a navigational note confirming the existence of a beam-bombing system: "Radio Beacon Knickebein from 06.00 hours on 315 degrees."

20 March   **Steamship 'Barnhill' sunk off Purbeck.**

Shipping in the Channel has again been attacked by bombers from Kampfgruppe 26. The 5,439-ton freighter SS *Barnhill* sank off the Isle of Purbeck. The crew escaped by lifeboat.

31 March   **Paper into shells at Holton Heath.**

Paper is being consumed by the Royal Naval Cordite Factory at Holton Heath and made into nitro cellulose. This guncotton pulp is mixed with nitroglycerine; the basis of cordite SC which is the propellant for the Navy's shells.

The factory has used 4,279,141 pounds of paper in the past year. That is 1,910 tons.

12 April   **Narvik wreath at Hardy Monument.**

A laurel wreath hangs on the door of the Hardy Monument, the memorial to Nelson's flag captain on the hills above Portesham — the village known to Thomas Hardy as "Possum" — in memory of the men of the Royal Navy who lost their lives two days ago in Narvik fjord, Norway.

A card reads: "To the unfading memory of Captain Warburton-Lee, RN, HMS *Hardy*, and the gallant men who died at Narvik. Nelson's Hardy and Hardy's Possum salute you."

The commemorative tower is now owned by the National Trust.

Footnote Bernard Warburton-Lee would be posthumously awarded the Victoria Cross.

24 April   **Holton Heath munitions factory hit.**

An oil incendiary bomb exploded at 22.10 hours tonight beside the wash-water settling house of the nitroglycerine complex at the Royal Naval Cordite Factory, Holton Heath. The wooden settling house began burning but Walt Dominey and his fire-fighting team brought the fire under control and averted a major disaster.

4 May   **Two Poole flying-boats destroyed in Norway.**

Two Short "Empire" flying-boats, the *Cabot* and *Caribou*, which had been seconded to 119 Squadron at Invergordon, have been attacked at anchor by a Heinkel He115 floatplane in Bodo fjord. They had arrived today to bring radar equipment to the beleagured British troops at Harstadt in northern Norway.

Footnote The equipment was lost in the attack though the injured crews were rescued and brought home by a British destroyer. A further raid, the following morning, sank the planes. They had been scheduled to operate BOAC's peacetime Atlantic service in 1940.

5 May   **Telecommunications Research Establishment moves to Worth Matravers.**

The Air Ministry's Telecommunications Research Establishment, which has pioneered the development of early warning radio-direction finding equipment known as radar, has been evacuated from Dundee to Dorset.

It is being housed in a hutted encampment on a plateau beside Renscombe Farm, a short distance from Chapman's Pool, at Worth Matravers in the Isle of Purbeck.

Telecommunications Research Establishment was previously known as the Air Ministry Research Establishment and used to be based at Bawdsey in pre-war days. It is headed by A.P. Rowe and Robert Watson-Watt.

Footnote RDF, originally the initials for Radio Direction Finding, came to be regarded as Range and Direction Finding but both would be replaced by the American description Radio Direction and Ranging, thanks to its catching palidrome mnemonic—radar.

8 May   **Special Duties Flight arrives at Christchurch.**

The Air Ministry's Special Duties Flight is arriving at Christchurch Aerodrome from St Athan, near Barry, in Glamorgan. It at present comprises six Ansons, four Blenheims, two Harrows, two Fairey Battles, and three adapted "Special Aircraft". These are a Hurricane, an Anson, and a High Altitude Machine.

The aeroplanes, which are to be augmented by other arrivals of a variety of types, carry experimental radar aerials and other items of secret equipment. They will be at the disposal of the Christchurch-based Air Defence and Research Development Establishment and scientists of the Telecommunications Research Establishment at Worth Matravers.

10 May   **2nd Dorsets in the Belgian front-line.**

The 2nd Battalion of the Dorsetshire Regiment, in the Belgian front-line to the east of Genval, awoke this morning to the drone of enemy aeroplanes and have been told to prepare for battle.

10 May   **Attlee recalled to London from Bournemouth.**

Labour leaders Clement Attlee and Arthur Greenwood have been recalled to London today from their party conference in Bournemouth, as the Chamberlain government is in crisis following the invasion of the Low Countries. Chamberlain has offered them positions in a new national government.

They have accepted the posts (Attlee as Lord Privy Seal; Greenwood as Minister without Portfolio) but rejected Chamberlain's continued leadership — which with Parliament's present mood will cause the Premier's instant resignation and a call to Winston Churchill to form the new government.

10 May   **Churchill's Dorset ancestry.**

With the fall today of Neville Chamberlain's government and Mr Churchill's appointment as Premier it is noted with approval in Dorset that his most distinguished ancestor, John Churchill, the first Duke of Marlborough, was the son of Winston Churchill of Round Chimneys Farm, Glanvilles Wootton, "of a good Dorset family". Winston Spencer Churchill is the grandson of the seventh Duke of Marlborough.

Last year his son, Randolph, married the Hon. Pamela Digby of Minterne Magna.

14 May   **Three thousand Dutch refugees camp on Brownsea.**

Following the sudden Nazi invasion into the Low Countries, which also delivered the coup de grace to the Chamberlain government, an armada of dozens of overloaded Dutch vessels is being shepherded by the Royal Navy into Poole Harbour. The refugees will be temporarily camped on Brownsea Island where they can be properly screened by doctors, police and the security services before being admitted into the country.

An estimated three thousand are on their way.

16 May   **2nd Dorsets withdraw towards France.**

"Où est la route pour France?" a Dorsetman heard as Algerian troops were beaten back by the German advance and the 2nd Battalion of the Dorsetshire Regiment found itself under further orders to withdraw in the face of overwhelming odds.

19 May   **2nd Dorsets see civilians bombed and strafed.**

For the first time the Dorset soldiers serving in Belgium, now pulled back to Tournai near the French border, have seen the bodies of civilians who were bombed and strafed by German aircraft. The town is on fire.

24 May   **2nd Dorsets invited to surrender.**

With German radio announcing that the ring around the French, Belgian and British armies has "definitely closed" the 2nd Battalion of the Dorsetshire Regiment — now withdrawn to La Bassée, south-west of Lille — has been showered from the air with leaflets inviting desertion: "You are surrounded — why fight on? We treat our prisoners well."

29 May   **Observers told not to fraternise with Local Defence Volunteers.**

Too much fraternisation is taking place with other civilian units, Dorset's local commander of the Observer Corps, Wing Commander Stewart, has told his men: "Head observers must consult their officers before making any commitments with the Local Defence Volunteers. No instruction has been received with regard to co-operation and any tendency to mingle at posts should be discouraged."

31 May   **Churchill flies from Warmwell to Paris.**

Prime Minister Winston Churchill has flown in a twin-engined de Havilland Flamingo transport aircraft from Warmwell Aerodrome to Paris for secret discussions on the deteriorating military situation. Nine Hurricanes from 601 (County of London) Squadron were deployed to escort the Premier's aeroplane. They waited overnight to bring it safely home.

Churchill met the French Premier and talked with Major-General Edward Spears, the British Prime Minister's personal representative with the French government and armed forces. The clutch of young pilots, even after their night on the town, reminded him of "the angels of my childhood".

Among those escort pilots was Flying Officer William Rhodes-Moorhouse, whose father was the first airman to win the Victoria Cross, in 1915, and is buried on a Dorset hillside, at Parnham above Beaminster.

Footnote As is son Willie. He was awarded the Distinguished Flying Cross during the Battle of Britain and would be killed in Hurricane P8818 during a complex dog-fight with Messerschmitt Bf109s above Tonbridge, Kent, on 6 September 1940. 601 Squadron grieved, and lost its aggressive spirit, according to Squadron Leader Max Aitken.

War artist Captain Cuthbert Orde wrote that all were affected from the commanding officer to the humblest aircraftman: "They couldn't believe it — it just couldn't have happened. His extraordinary combination of gaiety, joie de vivre, personal attraction and fighting qualities was something that just didn't disappear suddenly."

31 May   **2nd Dorsets evacuated from Dunkirk.**

After five days and nights of marching and fighting as they made their way north towards the Channel coast, the main contingent of the 2nd Battalion of the Dorsetshire Regiment last night completed an orderly withdrawal, under fire, to the Mole at Dunkirk where they boarded a Thames dredger. They were appalled to see that she seemed to be half-full of water but heard that dredgers are always like that.

May   **Local Defence Volunteers: six Dorset units.**

Major-General Harry Marriot-Smith is organising the Local Defence Volunteers under instructions from the War Office. Dorset is being covered by six battalions.

Footnote Churchill would have them renamed — the Home Guard. The 3rd Dorset Battalion was later split to create another, the 7th (Wareham) Battalion, and a Motor Transport Company was also formed as part of the Hants and Dorset Transport Column.

1 June   **Fleeing French troops arrive in Weymouth.**

The first train carrying Free French soldiers into Weymouth arrived at 05.00 hours. They are being taken to the former Christ Church, opposite the station, which has been converted into a refugee Welcome Club. There they are being issued with their first rations, half a loaf and a tin of bully-beef, and dispersed to various schools, halls and private accommodation.

2 June   **Hardy and love of England.**

Thomas Hardy was a patriot, speakers emphasised at the ceremony in Dorchester to mark the centenary of the author's birth. It was held beside his memorial statute in Colliton Walks today, Sunday, though the precise anniversary is Tuesday 4 June. Earl Baldwin of Bewdley, the former Conservative Prime Minister, laid a wreath and commented that he himself felt reservations during the week that the celebration should be postponed.

On further consideration, however, he thought there was nothing unseemly even at a moment like the present for English people to gather together in the part of England made famous by a very great Englishman to express their sense of what they owed to him. He had for many increased their knowledge and love of England, for which her sons today were laying down their lives.

4 June   **Poole and Weymouth craft help evacuate Dunkirk.**

Pleasure craft from Poole and Weymouth are in the armada of Operation Dynamo that today completed the evacuation of the British Expeditionary Force from the beaches of Dunkirk.

Among the craft taken to Dover from Poole were Harvey's *Ferry Nymph* and *Southern Queen; Davis's Felicity and Island Queen;* Bolson's *Skylarks VI, VIII and IX;* and *Thomas Kirk-Wright,* the harbour's inshore lifeboat. These craft were commandeered by the navy and the lifeboat, with its shallow draught, has the distinction of being used to go into the beaches. She has survived shore-fire from Germans positioned less than forty yards away.

The pleasure craft have proved ideal for taking aboard soldiers by the dozen but Poole's fishing fleet, which had also loyally turned up in response to the Admiralty's appeal, was summarily rejected by the navy. Its boatmen, who consider themselves to be the port's only true seamen, were sent home by train and their vessels impounded for possible reserve uses. They are unsuitable for this kind of mass transit.

A third of the 330,000 soldiers who have been brought out are French and 6,000 of these, from Flanders, have been sent to Weymouth. At Dorchester, however, the concern has been of a civilian influx, with news of a further 2,300 evacuees earmarked for the district. Only now are air-raid shelters being constructed in the town.

Footnote Of the local boats, the *Island Queen* and *Southern Queen* were sunk off Dunkirk, and *Skylark VI* abandoned with bomb damage. She was later salvaged, towed back to Bolson's shipyard at Poole and refitted with a larger engine as an Air-Sea Rescue craft. The fishermen returned by train for their boats a few days later.

9 June   Germans mine the channel into Poole.

Last night the Germans mined the Swash Channel that leads into the entrance to Poole Harbour, in anticipation of its use in some relief operation to bring out the beleagured units of the British Army struggling in Normandy.

12 June   Poole boats rescue troops from St Valery.

Overall, Operation Cycle failed to live up the Admiralty's expectations of a second mini-Dunkirk, but for some of the small Poole boats taking part it was a triumph. They last night played a key role in bringing 3,321 soldiers, a third of them British, from the salient at St Valery-en-Caux.

This time the Germans were ready for a maritime rescue mission, though it was the fog that disrupted the efforts of the early hours of the 11th and sent six thousand Scottish troops into prisoner-of-war camps. As part of their counter-measures the Germans mined the Swash Channel into Poole Harbour. It has been rendered at least partly clear by navy divers from Portland.

Not completely, however, as the *Princess Juliana*, found. She was sailing out of Poole last night when she hit a mine off the Training Bank and was lifted clear of the water. George Brown, the pilot, was rescued together with three of the Dutch crewmen.

Footnote Ivor Holland, instrumental in the rescue of *Princess Juliana*'s survivors, was to be awarded the Order of the Red Lion by the Netherlands.

13 June   Eleven killed as 'Abel Tasman' is blown up off Poole.

Three of the fifteen craft returning from St Valery with remnants of the British and French armies successfully ran the gauntlet of the Swash Channel into Poole Harbour today. The fourth and unlucky craft was *the Abel Tasman,* fortunately returning empty. She hit a mine and was blown to pieces, killing all eleven of her complement from the Royal Navy Volunteer Reserve. An order was then flashed to the remaining ships to turn and sail to Southampton.

13 June   'British Inventor' mined off St Alban's Head.

The steam tanker *British Inventor* struck a mine off St Alban's Head. Although she stayed afloat long enough to be put under tow the line had to be released as the stricken vessel began to go under.

Channels into the ports of Weymouth and Poole are being kept open through the efforts of two Portland-based minesweepers, HMS *Kindred Star* and HMS *Thrifty.*

15 June   **Swash Channel has first magnetic mines.**

The mines that have claimed two ships in recent days in the Swash Channel at the outer entrance to Poole Harbour include some, at least, of a new magnetic type that explode when they come close to a steel ship. These C-type mines have not yet been retrieved intact for examination and today the first attempt burst into a spectacular failure on Studland beach.

Harold Cartridge with the Poole fishing boat *Smiling Through*, under navy orders, managed to tow one on a seven hundred foot line from the Bar Buoy to the shallows of Studland beach — where for some unknown reason it decided to explode, though without more than a shock and a shake for Cartridge and his craft.

Footnote The Germans were slow in deploying this potentially devastating weapon. The first to be dismantled by the British would be recovered from Shoeburyness, Essex, on 22 November; the Germans had been lax in not incorporating an anti-handling device.

19 June   **Highcliffe sighting of French refugees.**

Two boats, apparently carrying French troophs fleeing from Cherbourg, have been spotted by the Local Defence Volunteers from their Highcliffe lookout; the Cliff Top Cafe. The craft are heading for Steamer Point, Christchurch.

20 June   **First air raid warning.**

Condition Red: this is the first air-raid warning at Christchurch, though there have been earlier alerts for Condition Yellow, the precautionary message from Fighter Command that enemy air activity is to be expected. With Condition Red the activity has been monitored and appears to be coming our way — it is a warning to take to the shelters, given as a two-minute warbling blast on the sirens.

Later there was a continuous two-minute wail from the siren to declare that it was All Clear. Nothing, thank God, happened in the interim.

Footnote Christchurch would experience 956 air raid warnings, the vast majority of them being of as little consequence. The last would be on 15 July 1944.

20 June   **Weymouth tears as the French leave.**

Tearful farewells marked Weymouth's parting with the French soldiers, the last of whom have now left to resume the war with fighting units. They were taken to heart, in a way that perhaps the Londoners and others weren't — but the town has experienced an influx unprecedented for anywhere in England. John Murphy has recorded one sad incident where a Catholic priest tried to say something kind to an unhappy Belgian woman but utterly failed.

"Are they all yours?" joked Father Jules Ketele when he saw she had three children with her. A good Catholic should have known better!

She burst into tears and sobbed that she had seven children when she left home eight days ago; those were all she had left.

The total number of arrivals for the past week has been 27,400 refugees, of which the bulk — 23,743 of them — have come from the Channel Islands which faces impending German invasion.

Footnote The Germans took over the Channel Islands at the end of the month, on 30 June and 1 July.

21 June   Christchurch Ansons fly in search of the 'beam'.

The Telecommunications Research Establishment, Worth Matravers, has organised a special mission tonight for three Anson aeroplanes from the Special Duties Flight at Christchurch. They will try, in poor weather,to use American radar receivers, to trackthe course of a German radio direction signal, intended to aid the navigation of bombers, that appears to lead from Spalding, Lincolnshire, and cross with another similar "beam" above the Rolls-Royce aero-engine factory at Derby. The Anson tracking this signal is being flown by Flight-Lieutenant H.E. Bufton, with Corporal Mackie as radio operator.

Footnote The Special Counter Measures Unit was to function as part of 109 Squadron.

23 June   Wooden glider blips on Worth's radar.

A British Avro 504N biplane today took off from Christchurch Aerodrome to tow a German Minimoa glider into the middle of the English Channel and released the wooden craft at 10,000 feet for it to glide back towards Purbeck. The glider pilot, Philip Wills, returned below cliff level at St Alban's Head and prepared for impact but was saved by the phenomenon of currents rising beside vertical surfaces.

The object of the exercise was for the Telecommunications Research Establishment at Renscombe, Worth Matravers, to establish with its radio direction finding aerials [RDF, now known as radar] whether short-wave radiation that bounced off metal bombers would also reflect from wooden gliders. Worth houses the country's principal radio research unit.

The answer was affirmative; to the relief of the scientists as the country is in fear of a mass invasion of German gliders. As for the Avro 504, it dates back to the beginning of the Great War, having been used in the first organised bombing raid — that on the Zeppelin sheds at Friedrichshafen, Lake Constance, on 21 November 1914.

25 June   69th Infantry Brigade takes over at Poole.

The 69th Infantry Brigade, late of France and the Dunkirk beaches, is now back in the front-line — at Poole and east Dorset where it has taken over the anti-invasion defences from the Queen's Bays. The Officer Commanding, Brigadier Barstow, is at Bovington Camp.

The Brigade comprises the 7th Battalion of the Green Howards, the 5th Battalion of the East Yorkshire Regiment and the 6th Battalion of the

Green Howards, who are dispersed into the countryside. The Adjutant of the Green Howards has found that the unit no longer possesses a duplicator — and is to ask Poole Corporation if he may borrow theirs.

June   Anti-ship guns emplaced around Poole Bay.

The 554th Coast Regiment of the Royal Artillery, with its headquarters at the Conningtower, West Road, Canford Cliffs, has sited naval guns, taken from warships and armed merchantmen at the end of the Great War and put into store, as the teeth of the anti-ship defences in Poole Bay.

The positions are: Two x 6-inch guns, Battery Hill, Brownsea Island — 347th Battery. Two x 5.5-inch guns, Hengistbury Head — 172nd Battery. Two x 6-inch guns, Mudeford — 175th Battery. Two x 4-inch guns, Swanage — 386th Battery.

Each set of emplacements has a complement of about a hundred men.

June   Ship and boom defence for Poole Harbour entrance.

An Examination Ship is positioned in the Swash Channel at the entrance to Poole Harbour. The duty is being undertaken by the ex-Belgian trawler *Rose Arthur,* now His Majesty's Trawler XVI, with her sister craft HMT XVII (*Roger Robert*) and HMT XVIII (*Marguerita Marie Louisa*). The alert code for the sighting of enemy forces is "Blackbird". That for a landing of troops is "Gallipoli" For a landing of tanks it is "Caterpillar".

Once a warning of invasion had been radioed and received on the mainland the craft's duty is to suspend the watching brief with a final signal — "Finish" — and head to sea to intercept enemy vessels.

As for the harbour entrance, it has a steel boom with suspended torpedo heads that have been provided by the Royal Naval Cordite Factory at Holton Heath. There is a passage open at the centre in daytime but in the evening this is closed by boatman George Mitchell.

Inside the harbour six pleasure craft have been requisitioned by the Royal Navy and armed with machine guns. They are HI to H6; the boats of the Poole Harbour Patrol.

In the Main Channel of Poole Harbour an old steamship, the *Empire Sentinel,* has been packed with explosives and in the event of invasion the harbour patrol will sink her to block the approaches to the port. Their prime duty is to ensure the closure of this channel.

Footnote Only one of the pleasure boats, *Etrillita* in civilian days, was retained as a patrol craft. The others were phased out and replaced.

June   British mines laid in Poole Harbour.

The Naval Officer-in-Command, Poole, is completing the laying of a minefield between Sandbanks and Brownsea Island to prevent the intrusion of German submarines or surface vessels. Anti-tank "islands" of urban coastal areas impregnable to tank attack have been established behind concrete obstacles, minefields and flame traps at the Old Town in Poole and at Christchurch. The Garrison Headquarters is also strongly defended in the centre of Bournemouth.

The whole of the area from Upton to Mudeford is under the control of the Garrison Commander at Bournemouth.

June   **Royal Naval Air Station Sandbanks.**

Seaplane training for Fleet Air Arm pilots is now based at Poole, from the middle of this month, with the removal from Calshot on Southampton Water to Sandbanks of 765 Squadron, the Royal Navy Seaplane School. At Calshot they had been heavily bombed.

The squadron trains its pilots on the air-sea rescue Walrus, which is distinctive with a chugging sound and floats on its wings. It is known as the "Shagbat".

On the Sandbanks slipway the machines are stored with their wheels down and wings folded back. The unit also has the Swordfish torpedo-reconnaissance biplane, known as the "Stringbag," and Kingfisher and Seafox floatplanes.

The base is known as Royal Navy Air Station Sandbanks.

Footnote But to Poole people it was HMS Tadpole — because it handled beginners with seaplanes that were dwarfed by the flying-boats operating from the harbour with BOAC and Coastal Command. The name was later adopted by the Navy for real, in 1943, for a preinvasion landing craft training establishment.

June   **Bovington's tank collection scrapped or used as pillboxes.**

The collection of the world's first tanks at the Armoured Fighting Vehicles School, Bovington Camp, has been dispersed to help the war effort. Many have been taken away for scrap and others are in strategic positions as stationary pill-boxes.

The vehicles had been put in a shed after Rudyard Kipling visited Bovington in 1923 and expressed disappointment that nothing was being done to preserve them.

June   **Four hundred French soldiers rest in Bournemouth.**

As the exhausted armies are dispersed from the reception ports a detachment of four hundred French soldiers is told to go to Bournemouth for a short recuperation whilst billets are located. Canon Hedley Burrows found they had been sent to St Peter's Hall in the centre of the town.

He telephoned the Town Clerk to ask who was in charge of these men. "You are!" he was told. Canon Burrows is arranging their accommodation.

Thousands more are to pass through Bournemouth like refugees. It is said the only fully equipped division in Britain is Canadian.

1 July   **Ration books and identity cards.**

Ration books for food came into force today, with green coupons for meat, yellow for butter and margarine, and orange for cooking fat.

Identity cards are being issued to all those living in the Military Control areas, which in Dorset include the entire coast and its towns and stretch twenty miles inland. The Commissioner responsible for the control of civilians in the South-West Region is Sir Geoffrey Peto but the National Registration Identity Cards, each carrying the individual's photograph, are issued locally. In the case of Sandbanks, for instance, they will be signed by the Officer Commanding Troops, Poole Defence Area.

Those without cards have to give reasons for entry into the Military Control areas when they encounter vehicle check points and police also carry out spot-checks inside the zone on bus passengers and in public places.

2 July — Green Howards wiring up the Bournemouth beaches.

All beach chalets and huts are to be removed from the beaches of Bournemouth and Poole, having been considered to have been requisitioned by the military. Their clearance has been demanded to ensure a proper field of fire across the sands. Wire barriers are to be erected by the Green Howards along the low-tide line and emplacements built at intervals. Particular strong points will be at the Haven Hotel and Sandbanks Pavilion. Sandbanks is being sealed-off.

3 July — Bournemouth gets its first bomb.

Southampton received its first enemy bombers early on 19 June and today, at 00.12 hours, came Bournemouth's turn. A single high-explosive bomb fell at Cellars Farm Road, Southbourne. It set a house on fire and damaged eighteen other properties.

The explosion and blaze caused considerable consternation. Rumours followed and at 02.45 hours, on the other side of the River Stour, Christchurch police issued a warning that German parachutists had landed.

4 July — Control points surround Sandbanks.

Effectively, from today, Sandbanks at Poole is sealed with military control points in operation at Shore Road and the Haven Hotel crossing point, and on the Studland road at Shell Bay. From the 6th the position will be regularised by the issue of permits to the 544 inhabitants who will have to gather at the Haven Hotel to have their photographs taken and undergo an interview before they are accredited with official clearance documents.

4 July — Dozens killed and Portland hero keeps firing as he dies.

Ninety Junkers Ju87 "Stukas" today attacked Convoy OA178 between Portland and Hengistbury Head, sinking the steamship *Elmcrest* and three other vessels. A further nine ships were damaged.

The dive-bombers then attacked Portland Harbour where they sank two ships, including the anti-aircraft auxiliary HMS *Foylebank*. A dozen "Stukas" came at her and one of the first casualties was 23-year-old Leading Seaman Jack Mantle who went to school at Affpuddle but was recently living in Southampton. Despite having his legs shattered as bombs tore the ship apart, causing loss of electrical power, he stayed at his pom-

pom and continued firing even as he suffered further wounds, and must have known he was mortally injured.

Fifty-nine of his comrades were also killed and a total of sixty were injured—the other sixty somehow came out of it unscathed.

Perhaps the unluckiest people on Portland that day were nine contractors from McAlpine's, who had been digging a tunnel. They sheltered inside it during the raid and came out when it was thought to be over; to be killed by a last bomb from a single German plane that turned back from the sea. Four of those workers were boys.

Footnote There were repercussions. The Admiralty closed the English Channel to ocean-going merchant vessels, though coastal convoys would continue.

Jack Mantle was gazetted with the first Victoria Cross that the Royal Navy had won inside territorial waters. He is buried in Portland's Naval Cemetery on the Verne Common hillside.

Open air gatherings were henceforth restricted. Only family mourners could attend the funerals that resulted from the day's events. At one the Fortuneswell Methodist minister, Rev F. Jowett, said: "We owe a tribute of gratitude and affection to the one who has departed. He has given his life for his King and country, and those things for which we Englishmen stand."

5 July   **E-boats maul Convoy OA 178.**

The remnants of Convoy OA 178, which suffered considerably from a Junkers Ju87 "Stukas" onslaught yesterday, were harassed last night by E-boats, German Schnellboote, off Poole Bay. One ship has sunk and two more are damaged.

Footnote E-boat was the German term "Eil-Boot" meaning "Fast Boat" — specifically Schnellboot (plural Schnellboote), the German motor torpedoboat (or S-Boat).

5 July   **'Hartlepool' sinks beside Weymouth Harbour entrance.**

SS Hartlepool, a British freighter, has sunk on the north-east side of the entrance to Weymouth Habour. The vessel had been crippled by German "Stuka" dive-bombers that attacked a convoy in the southern part of Weymouth Bay.

She was put in tow with the intention of beaching her on Weymouth sands but shipped too much water and went down in four fathoms little more than half-a-mile offshore. She lies to the north of the ship-channel into Weymouth Harbour; where she is less of a navigation hazard than might of been as her superstructure and mast remain visible at high tide.

Footnote The bow section was later pulled clear and removed for scrap but the stern and mast remained clearly visible from Weymouth beach until the winter of 1941. The wreck was then blown up.

5 July   **Bournemouth's piers are blown-up.**

In view of the possibilities they offer, not only for German airborne landings, but also as supply points for any conventional invasion force, the precaution has been taken of "blowing" the seaside piers at Bournemouth and Boscombe. The Royal Engineers today carried out a series of explosions to demolish the central sections of both piers.

The seaward ends, the scene of the famous end-of-the-pier shows, are being left as islands. It is a sad epitaph to those years of joy and a reminder, not that one is now needed, of the state of siege that has descended upon southern England. It is going to shock anyone who cherishes memories of the Victorian bathchairs.

6 July   **Warmwell taken over by Fighter Command.**

Fighter aircraft are to be based close to the central Dorset coast in order to counter the Luftwaffe's increasing threat to Channel shipping and in direct response to its audcacious attack on the Royal Navy base at Portland. The Deputy Chief of the Air Staff, Air Vice-Marshal W. Sholto Douglas, issued the order and today RAF Warmwell has become a front-line defensive aerodrome with the arrival of the Spitfires of 609 (West Riding) Squadron under Squadron Leader Horace Stanley "George" Darley.

The Squadron code letters are "PR". Control of the airfield has been transferred to No. 10 Group of Fighter Command, the headquarters of which is at Box, near Bath, and its sector base and home aerodrome is Middle Wallop, near Andover, Hampshire. The pilots return there in the evening and come back to Dorset the following morning.

Scramble time is fifteen minutes and the accommodation is tented.

The advent of the eight-gun fighter has revolutionised aerial warfare. There were 187 Spitfires in squadron service on the Sunday war was declared — by the end of that month 4,000 were on order and their production has the highest priority.

Footnote There was an inflexible meals timetable at Warmwell that often caused friction and Darley would damn Dorset for its treatment of his men. Once he started the day with a row with the cooks and had to prepare his own breakfast, breaking off to take to the sky to fight off some "Stukas". Back on the ground he rang the Station Commander to say he wished to be spared any thanks "for saving the hangars, personnel, and planes, not to mention the officers' mess and kitchens".

Lance Corporal Tony Hollister, later of Swanage, witnessed a gratuitous insult from an ex-Indian Army major to a couple of Warmwell pilots. "Take your bloody hands out of your pockets and salute a senior officer." They deflated him with unprintable public school drawl. There used to be a simple phrase for causing apoplexy amongst such persons: "I always regarded the terrorists as the cream of Bengal."

9 July   **Warmwell pilot and 'Stuka' leader killed off Portland.**

Dive-bombers today attacked Channel shipping off Portland and 609 Squadron was scrambled from Warmwell Aerodrome.

Three Warmwell Spitfires closed in on two Junkers Ju87 "Stukas" but then at least nine Messerschmitt Bf110s dived on the British fighters from above.

The attacking Bf110s were spotted by Pilot Officer David Moore Crook in Spitfire P9322 (PR-L).

He yelled a radio warning to his two companions. Pilot Officer Michael Appleby switched his radio from transmit just in time to be told "Messerschmitts" and pull his Spitfire clear.

The third Spitfire, flown by Pilot Officer Peter Drummond-Hay, must still have had its radio on transmit and was lost in the action over the sea.

Then, David Crook writes in his log: "I found myself very near to a Ju87 so stalked it through cloud and when it emerged into clear sky I fired all the rest of my ammunition at very close range. He turned over and dived in flames into the sea."

This dive-bomber was piloted by Hauptmann Friedrich-Karl Freiherr von Dalwigk zu Lichtenfels, the 33-year-old Staffelkapitän of I Gruppe, Stukageschwader 77. Their code letter and number are S2.

Footnote Von Dalwigk, who had joined the Luftwaffe in 1933, would be posthumously awarded the Knight's Cross on 21 July 1940.

9 July   **Poole now a sealed-off town.**

Poole is now part of the Defence Area, with access restricted to those with reason for entering the town, under a regulation signed by Regional Controller Harold Butler.

10 July   **Poole flying-boat arrives in Sydney.**

The British Empire's air link resumed today with the arrival in Sydney of a BOAC flying-boat from Poole. Another has reached Durban. They have flown a horseshoe-shaped route to Lisbon and across the southern Sahara.

The Australian plane then travelled northwards via Khartoum and Cairo on to the usual peacetime flight path across Palestine, the Persian Gulf, India and Malaya.

The route to South Africa is via Lagos and Leopoldville.

11 July   **Anti-glider precautions erected at Poole.**

Among the various anti-landing traps being laid to discourage enemy glider forces are rows of telegraph poles which are being cut into sections and dug into the fairways of Parkstone golf links and across Branksome playing fields. The poles are ten feet apart and form rows every hundred yards.

11 July   **Two more Warmwell losses and a German crashes near Lulworth.**

Two more Spitfires from Warmwell's 609 Squadron have been lost in action over the English Channel, whilst fighting off a "Stuka" bombardment of a convoy of British merchant ships.

The attacks were in Lyme Bay, by fifty enemy aircraft, and 609 Squadron went to the aid of the hard-pressed Hurricanes from Exeter which had battled alone against an attack earlier in the day by twenty bombers and forty fighters. The steam yacht *Warrior II* was sunk in the first attack and another ship damaged in the second raid.

It is reported that as a result of this action a Messerschmitt Bf110 has crashed on Povington Heath, between East Lulworth and East Holme, and that this is the first German aircraft to be brought down on Dorset soil.

The two Spitfire pilots who have failed to return to Warmwell are Flying Officer Philip Henry "Pip" Barran in L1096 and Pilot Officer Gordon Thomas Manners Mitchell in L1095 Barran was picked up from the sea, five miles off Portland Bill, but was badly wounded and burnt, dying before he could be brought ashore.

11 July Tyneham Germans are first flyers to be taken prisoner.

The two enemy flyers in Messerschmitt Bf110 (2N+EP) brought down this afternoon on Povington Heath in the parish of Tyneham survived their crash landing and are the first Germans to be taken prisoner in the Battle of Britain. They are Oberleutnant Gerhard Kadow, pilot, and Gefreiter Helmut Scholz, gunner, of the 9th Staffel, Zerstorergeschwader 76.

They flew at noon from Laval, via a refuelling stop at Dinard, and were among the fighters escorting Junkers Ju87 "Stuka" dive-bombers that attacked Channel shipping off Portland.

Their two-engined aeroplane has twisted propellers and a dented underside but is otherwise undamaged.

The kill has been claimed by Warmwell Spitfires of 609 Squadron.

12 July More Spitfires for Warmwell.

An unblooded support squadron, 152 (Hyderabad) Squadron, has flown into Warmwell Aerodrome, led by Squadron Leader Peter Devitt who learnt to fly at the age of nineteen in 1930. Their markings are "UM". The squadron is equipped with Spitfires and has had its practice flights in the north of England.

It was originally formed on 1 October 1918 and has been operating from Acklington Aerodrome, Northumberland, since 2 October 1939.

12 July Northumberland Fusiliers to prepare Bournemouth's defences.

Veterans of Dunkirk, the 4th Battalion of the Royal Northumberland Fusiliers have arrived in Bournemouth after a short stay at Yeovil followed by a few days in tents at Piddlehinton. Here in the seaside resort they are taking over the coast defences from the Royal Artillery and will lay mines and erect wood, steel and concrete anti-invasion obstacles.

13 July 'Stay-put if the Germans invade' – mayors order.

Learning from the chaos brought to France and Belgium by refugees blocking the roads in the hours that preceded the arrival of the Germans, the mayors of the Bournemouth conurbation have emphasised that there is to be no civilian evacuation if the enemy invades.

All major roads would be sealed off for the use of the Army and if the enemy comes he will in the Bournemouth area take on the burden of an army of occupation with a quarter of a million population to control and support. Resistance will continue from the "fighting boxes" garrisoned by upwards of fifty armed men, and in some cases two hundred or more.

These, it is said, are "fortified, supplied and organised to withstand siege without outside assistance".

| 13 July | **German aircraft suffer in dog-fights off Portland.** |

Spitfires from 609 Squadron, whilst flying a convoy protection patrol over the English Channel, today encountered German aircraft at 15,000 feet off Portland. Flying Officer John Charles Dundas, in R6634, came out of the sun at a Messerschmitt Bf110 which he claimed to have destroyed, and had a dog-fight with other German fighter-bombers. He then landed at Warmwell Aerodrome.

Meanwhile, Pilot Officer Rogers Freeman Garland "Mick" Miller, in Spitfire L1065, took on and damaged a Bf110, and then found a Dornier. The coup de grace for the latter was executed by the Hurricanes of 238 Squadron from Middle Wallop on the Hampshire Downs.

Footnote Dundas's claimed Bf110 kill was not in fact destroyed but managed to limp back to France.

| 13 July | **Australian Hurricane pilot killed at West Knighton.** |

An Australian volunteer, Flying Officer John Connelly Kennedy from Sydney, was killed today when his damaged Hurricane P2950 failed to clear power lines that obstructed his attempted crash-landing at Little Mayne Farm, West Knighton.

It is thought he was wounded during the afternoon encounter off the Chesil Beach in which a Dornier Do17 (4U+DK) was intercepted by the Hurricanes of 238 Squadron, from Middle Wallop, and brought down. Kennedy turned towards Warmwell Aerodrome, to the north-east, but lost too much height and crashed two miles short of the airfield. He was twenty-three.

The identification markings of the Do17 indicate that it belonged to the 2nd Staffel of Aufklärungsgruppe 123, a reconnaissance unit.

| 16 July | **'I have decided to prepare a landing against England'
– Hitler.** |

Luftwaffe "Enigma" machine-coded radio messages have today carried a directive from Hitler. The translation of the deciphered intercept, passed to Churchill by the Government's Code and Cipher School at Bletchley Park, Buckinghamshire, reads: "I have decided to prepare a landing operation against England and if necessary to carry it out."

17 July   **Churchill visits the Dorset invasion coast.**

Winston Churchill today saw the invasion precautions along the most vulnerable beaches of the South Coast when he inspected units at Branksome Chine and Sandbanks. At Branksome he showed his skill as a bricklayer by making a practical contribution to the defences that are taking shape.

He recalled to General Alan Brooke, the chief of Southern Command who had driven with him from Gosport, that it was from the rustic bridge at Alum Chine that he had fallen twenty feet in 1892, at the age of seventeen, very nearly plunging to his death.

They dined at the Armoured Fighting Vehicles School, Bovington, and were at Wool Station at 20.00 hours for Churchill's train back to London. Brooke is less than confident with what he has seen, he confides to his diary: "What has been going on in this country since the war started . . . The ghastly part is that I feel certain that we can only have a few more weeks before the Boche attacks." For all that, he admitted, he realised it was imperative to "maintain a confident exterior".

Footnote Brooke was unimpressed by his men's equipment and means but Churchill realised he had a considerable asset in Brooke – two days later he was promoted Commander-in-Chief Home Forces; on Christmas Day 1941 he became Chief of the Imperial General Staff.

18 July   **Warmwell celebrates revenge.**

Warmwell's Spitfire pilots have returned with their first kills. Two enemy aircraft have been shot down by 609 Squadron, which has done much to restore morale after their own recent losses.

One of the kills, a Dornier bomber which crash-landed close to Fleet church, became the second German aircraft to be brought down in Dorset. It had been attacking shipping in Lyme Bay. The pilot, who was the only survivor, passed looted Players cigarettes to his captors.

On the other hand, 609 Squadron has lost another Spitfire, and has a second machine awash on a beach, but both pilots are safe. Flight-Lieutenant Frank Jonathan Howell parachuted into the sea from Spitfire R6634 during a mid-afternoon dog-fight five miles from Swanage. A Royal Navy launch picked him up, and also Flying Officer Alexander Rothwell Edge, whom they found on Studland beach.

He had brought Spitfire R6636 down on to the sands after machine-gun fire from a Junkers had smashed his engine cooling system. As the tide came in the fighter was covered by the sea.

Footnote R6636 was salvaged and would fly again.

20 July   **Warmwell pilot killed.**

Pilot Officer Frederick Hyam Posener, a 23-year-old   South African volunteer flying Spitfire K9880 from RAF Warmwell with 152 Squadron, has been shot down in an engagement with enemy aircraft off Swanage.

Only yesterday the squadron flew its first operational sortie from Warmwell Aerodrome.

21 July   Hurricanes shoot down Dornier at Blandford.

The Hurricanes of 238 Squadron from RAF Middle Wallop, claim the Dornier Do17 (5F+0M) which was shot down at 15.00 hours over Nutford Farm, Pimperne, a mile north of Blandford. Its three crew were wounded in the crash and taken into the farmhouse for treatment before being driven to hospital.

The "5F" identification markings on the enemy aircraft indicate that it belonged to Aufklärungsgruppe 14, a reconnaissance unit.

21 July   Norwegian tanker ablaze off Swanage.

Swanage Coastguard reported a vessel on fire, about ten miles out in the English Channel directly south of the town, at 18.15 hours this evening. The lifeboat *Thomas Markby* was launched at 18.27 from the slipway at Peveril Point and made good speed in a light sea.

She headed towards the distant smoke and found the Norwegian tanker *Kollskegg* burning towards the bow after being dive-bombed by the Luftwaffe. Her crew had already been taken off by a British destroyer. The lifeboat waited until a dockyard tug arrived on the scene to take the tanker in tow, and then sent a party aboard to assist in fastening the wires.

22 July   No 4 Commando formed at Weymouth.

No 4 Commando, which was formed in Weymouth earlier this month, today held its first parade, followed by the commanding officer's opening address, which was given in the Pavilion on the Esplanade.

Footnote Though it would spend only a few weeks training in south Dorset in the summer of 1940, the battalion returned to the Weymouth area in August 1942 to prepare for the Dieppe Raid.

24 July   400 killed in liner torpedoed off Portland.

The Vichy French liner *Meknès* has sunk after being torpedoed by German submarine U-572 off Portland. She was carrying 1,100 neutral French sailors, of whom 400 are estimated to have perished.

25 July   Two German planes and Spitfire shot down.

Squadron Leader Peter Devitt today led the Spitfires of 152 Squadron from Warmwell in their first successful interception. Calling "Tally ho!" and hearing an "Achtung, Spitfire" response his fighters attacked a Dornier with Junkers Ju87 "Stuka" dive-bombers over Portland.

The Dornier crashed near Weymouth, killing one of the crew, and a "Stuka" was seen plunging burning into the sea. Both kills were claimed by Ralph "Bob" Wolton flying UM-F for Freddie with the coup de grace being delivered to the Dornier by Flying Officer Edward Christopher "Jumbo"

Deanesley who then went after a "Stuka" but ended up baling out wounded as Spitfire K9901 crashed into the sea five miles south of Portland Bill. He was picked up by the SS *Empire Henchman* and dropped off at Lyme Regis.

26 July   E-boats sink three ships off Dorset.

An E-boat Flotilla, comprising three German motor torpedo boats – Schnellboote S19, S20 and S27 – have sunk three merchant vessels in attacks in the Channel between Portland and the Isle of Wight.

27 July   Warmwell Spitfire lost off Weymouth.

Pilot Officer James Richebourg Buchanan of 609 Squadron, flying Spitfire N3023 from Warmwell Aerodrome lost his life today over Weymouth Bay when his fighter was attacked by Messerschmitt Bf109s. He was aged 25.

29 July   Destroyer loss shock – Germans have radar.

HMS *Delight*, a 1,375-ton destroyer of the "Defender" class was today dive-bombed by Junkers Ju87 "Stukas" and sank twenty miles south of Portland Bill.

Footnote Shortly after she had gone down an intercepted German radio message in the "Enigma" code was deciphered by the British Code and Cipher School at Bletchley Park, Buckinghamshire. It stated that the warship "had been sunk with the aid of Freya reports".

"Freya" was the codename for some device. Her name was plucked from Norse mythology and Dr Reg Jones, head of scientific intelligence at the Air Ministry, had already heard of "Freya Gerat" (Freya apparatus).

Jones writes in *Most Secret War* that seeing a mention of "Freya-Meldung" (Freya reporting) on 5 July he had bought a book on myths from Foyle's and found that "Freya was the Nordic Venus who had not merely sacrificed, but massacred her honour to gain possession of a magic necklace, Brisinga-men. The necklace was guarded by Heimdall, the watchman of the Gods, who could see a hundred miles by day or night."

The last phrase is the crucial one – making Heimdall a wholly appropriate code for radar, though rather too obvious. Freya was chosen, by association, in its place.

Twelve days before the loss of *Delight*, Jones had used this reasoning to predict the existence "of a coastal chain and detecting system with a range of a hundred miles". The sinking of the destroyer removed any possibility that Freya was detecting associated objects in the sky – for *Delight* had neither balloon protection nor a fighter escort.

"The apparatus must have been able to detect her directly," Jones concluded. "It appeared to be sited near the village of Auderville on the Hague peninsula north-west of Cherbourg, but it had to be very different from our own coastal chain stations, since it was completely undetectable on the best air photographs that we possessed of the area.

"This confirmed the idea that Freya was a fairly small apparatus, which had already been suggested by the fact that it had been set up so quickly after the Germans had occupied the Channel coast." The story would resume on 24 February 1941 with the picking up of a German radar signal by a scientist from the Telecommunications Research Establishment from St Alban's Head, Worth Matravers.

29 July   **Admiralty bans Channel convoys and destroyers.**

The English Channel has been placed off-limits to destroyers in daytime as a result of today's loss of HMS *Delight*, twenty miles south of Portland Bill. It brings to four the losses of destroyers in the mid-Channel area this month – the others being HMS *Brazen*, *Codrington* and *Wren*.

Thirty-six merchant ships have also been sunk, five of them when Convoy CW8 was mauled by Junkers Ju87 "Stuka" dive-bombers. As a result of these awful losses the Admiralty suspended coastal convoys in the English Channel, as from two days ago.

July   **Dorset Heavy Regiment redesignated.**

The Dorset Heavy Regiment of the Royal Artillery, which includes the gunners responsible for the defence of the naval anchorage at Portland, has been reformed as the 522nd (Dorset) Coast Regiment. They have 9.2 inch guns in the batteries at East Weares, at 400-feet on the Portland cliffs, and on the other side of Weymouth Bay at Upton Fort, to the east of Osmington Mills.

July   **Warmwell is RAF station 'XW'.**

RAF Warmwell in the centre of south Dorset, at 207-feet above sea level on a featureless gravel plain four miles east-south-east of Dorchester, has been issued with the pundit code "XW". This is being displayed in huge white letters, ten-feet high, and will also be flashed in morse code at night, in red light, from a mobile beacon.

July   **Home Guard cover-up the Cerne Giant.**

Members of the Home Guard have dragged scrub and branches across the hillside north of Cerne Abbas to cover the famous 180-feet high chalk-cut figure of a naked man that is etched into the turf of the Dorset Downs. It was considered that this ancient curiosity, known as the Cerne Giant, might be of practical use as a navigation marker for German aircraft, particularly any making northward across the Dorset coast from Portland towards Bristol.

Likewise the prominent Devonshire marble obelisk on Ballard Down, above Swanage, has been toppled. It was originally a lamp standard in central London.

Local authority workmen are busily digging up milestones and taking down road signs so that German invaders will not find their routes spelt out on the ground. It will still, however, be relatively easy to identify the major conurbation as it would be impractical to remove all clues, such as the hundreds of cast-iron drain covers that proclaim "COUNTY BOROUGH OF BOURNEMOUTH".

July   **Boulogne award for Dorset hero.**

Major "Billy" Fox-Pitt, who was awarded the Military Cross for gallantry whilst commanding a Welsh Guards company at Ginchy on the Somme in 1916, has been gazetted for the Distinguished Service Order in recognition of his leadership and example in holding out against strong German armoured attacks for two days in the attempt to defend Boulogne. The two battalions of the 20th Guards Brigade had been sent to France at short notice.

Footnote Fox-Pitt would be ADC to the King, 1945-47, and in retirement in Dorset – at Marsh Court, Caundle Marsh – hunted with the Blackmore Vale until the age of 79; he died in 1988 at the age of 92.

July   **Poole camouflage requests rejected.**

The Air Ministry has turned down requests from Dorset County Council for the camouflaging of prominent buildings in Poole, saying that this would make attacks more likely: "Low flying aircraft would easily see these buildings even if they were camouflaged, and, if they were seen to be camouflaged they would be taken to be more important targets than they really were. Thus camouflaging them would attract attack rather than avoid it."

July   **'British Resistance' guerrilla hideouts in Dorset.**

Thirty-two underground hideouts have been established secretly by the Royal Engineers in woods and commons scattered through the Dorset countryside to conceal the weapons, explosives and food necessary for Auxiliary Units of British Resistance to operate behind German lines in the event of an invasion.

This is considered most likely to take place on the sandy beaches between Studland and Hurst Castle, with secondary landings perhaps in Lyme Bay. The plan is that these elite units of the Home Guard should have the local knowledge and connections to sustain a campaign of harassment against the occupying forces. Each unit is under the control of regular Army officers to ensure the necessary level of expertise and professionalism.

Footnote   Schoolboys from North Perrott would discover the bunker secreted just above the spring-line in a dense coppice west of Higher Meerhay Farm, below Mintern's Hill, north of Beaminster.

July   **Fascist Dorset landowner interned.**

A major Dorset landowner has been arrested and imprisoned with the round-up of pre-war members and supporters of Sir Oswald Mosley's British Union of Fascists. He is Captain George Henry Lane Fox Pitt-Rivers of Hinton St Mary, who was last in the news when he opposed the billeting of city children in rural Dorset. Pitt-Rivers is being held under Defence Regulation 18b.

Footnote By August there were 1,600 detained in prison without trial; three out of four of them were Mosley's members. All but four hundred would be released during the winter of 1940-41. Pitt-Rivers was among those who were still held.

4 August   **Poole flying-boat crosses the Atlantic.**

The Short "Empire" flying-boat *Clare*, which took off early yesterday from the "Trots" in Poole Harbour as the water runways are known, today landed on the east coast of the United States and thereby resumed the transatlantic service. She carried three American government VIPs and will return with ferry pilots.

The flying-boat's pilots are Captains J.C. Kelly Rogers and G.R.B. Wilcockson, with crew men White, Burgess and Rotherham.

Footnote See 14 August 1940 for *Clare* pictured on her return.

5 August   **French General leaves Poole to arrange a coup.**

Colonel René de Larminat, the high commissioner of Free French Africa, has flown from Poole in the "Empire" flying-boat *Clyde* to arrange a coup d'etat in the Vichy controlled French colonies in the Congo basin. They are flying via Lagos to Leopoldville in the Belgian Congo from where the general and his staff officers will begin their programme for the repossession of French Equitorial Africa.

Footnote The Free French Army, led by General Carretier, walked back to power after taking Brazzaville by complete surprise.

8 August   **More mines laid off Dorset.**

The Channel shipping lanes have been subject to further German minelaying in the past thirty-six hours. The Räumboote, armed motor minesweepers, the enemy's 3rd Mine Laying Flotilla have been active off Dorset, protected by Schnellboote of the 5th E-boat Flotilla.

8 August   **German and Warmwell losses as another convoy tries to get through.**

Convoy CW9 has broken through the enemy's blockade of the English Channel, westwards from the Thames, but with severe losses. Three ships were sunk and one damaged by E-boat attacks off the Isle of Wight and two Royal Navy destroyers were called out from Portsmouth to give help. An air attack by sixty planes was intercepted and driven off but the convoy then fell victim to a second wave of more than 130 enemy aircraft off Bournemouth.

Here three more ships were lost and thirteen damaged. The Germans lost fourteen aircraft.

Spitfire K9894 of 152 Squadron was damaged in the dog-fights and headed for home. It crashed at Bestwall, on the east side of Wareham, but Sergeant Pilot Denis Norman Robinson had a miraculous escape. The fuselage ended up standing vertically, with the propeller embedded in the meadow, and Robinson was able to jump down on to the grass. Another Spitfire of 152 Squadron was successfully brought down by Pilot Officer Walter Beaumont in a field at Spyway Farm, on top of the Purbeck cliffs at Langton Matravers.

10 August   Bournemouth cyclist killed in air-raid.

Bombs fell last night on Bournemouth. At 47 Alyth Road, which was demolished at 23.24 hours, the disrobed lady of the house fell back into the safety of her bath as the roof collapsed.

Less fortunate was a cyclist in Meon Road where five high explosive bombs dropped at about 06.30 this morning. He was killed. Thirty-eight houses suffered damage.

11 August   Big air-raid on Weymouth and Portland.

A massed formation of Luftwaffe bombers and fighters, estimated to consist of more than 150 aircraft, was plotted by Ventnor radar as it gathered over the Cherbourg peninsula at 09.45 hours.

They then crossed the Channel with some ninety Messerschmitt Bf 109s and Bf110s sweeping towards Portland from the south-east, to clear the way for fifty Junkers Ju88s and twenty Heinkel He111s.

The dive-bombers swooped from 10,000 feet at around 10.30, dropping 32 bombs inside Admiralty property at Portland and three on the Royal Naval Torpedo Depot at Bincleaves, Weymouth. A total of 58 bombs fell in the borough. Quite a number also fell in the open sea, Portland Harbour and Balaclava Bay.

Almost everywhere it was the same story of near misses and lucky escapes. Though appearing to be more serious, a fire beside No.3 oil-tank at Portland was contained, and the adjoining blaze that made the beach road impassable was due to burning grass.

The main pipeline was fractured in three places with the loss of about 200-tons of oil. About the only other serious damage was to the shipwright's shop at Bincleaves which received a direct hit.

11 August   Five Bf110s claimed by Warmwell's Spitfires.

Five twin-engined Messerschmitt Bf110s were accounted for this morning by the Spitfires of 609 Squadron from RAF Warmwell, in a fast-moving action that swirled high above Portland from 10.10 to 10.35.

Pilot Officer David Moore Crook, flying R6986 (PR-S), records in his log: "We took off at 09.45 and after patrolling round Warmwell saw some smoke trails out to sea. Investigated and found a large force of Bf110s flying round in circles at 25,000 feet, Hurricanes already engaging them. We all attacked separately. I climbed well above the scrum and then saw a Bf110 some distance from the others. I dived on him and fired a burst from the rear quarter which missed as I could not get sufficient deflection. I then came into very close range and fired. I hit him and he did a climbing turn to the right, stalled and started to turn over. I narrowly missed colliding with him and did not see him again. Found myself with Messerschmitts all around so dived away as hard as I could and returned to Warmwell."

Most of the kills fell into the sea, but one crashed near Swanage. It has been credited to Flying Officer John Dundas, whose Spitfire, R6769, took shots through the starboard wing and rudder from the gunner of the stricken Bf110.

11 August   **Junkers lands on Portland.**

Flying Officer James Murray Strickland, in a Hurricane of 213 Squadron from RAF Exeter, bagged a twinengined Junkers Ju88 (B3+DC) in style this afternoon. The German pilot almost succeeded in bringing his crippled bomber down upon "The Castles" as the Portlanders call the flat top of the 275-feet cliffs at Blacknor Fort, Portland. This spot overlooks Lyme Bay from the centre of the western side of the stony island.

The sheer cliffs and the rocks were outmanoeuvred but not the fort's line of telephone wires. These retracted the undercarriage. The pilot was seriously hurt as the aircraft bounced to a halt but his three comrades had only superficial injuries. The markings "B3" indicate that the Ju88 belonged to Kampfgeschwader 54, a bomber wing whose death's head emblem — Totenkopf — appeared on the fuselage just aft of the transparent nose.

By the end of the day there was also serious damage to 213 Squadron. Two Hurricanes had been lost, with their pilots. Two other Hurricanes had made forced landings though both their pilots were unhurt and the machines repairable.

Sergeant Pilot Ernest Snowden of 213 Squadron brought P3585 down on to 'C' Range at Lulworth Camp. The engine had been hit by return fire from a Bf110 which he was shooting down. The second damaged Hurricane managed to limp back to Exeter.

Hurricane P3598 of 87 Squadron also crash-landed in Dorset, not quite making it to Warmwell Aerodrome, and injured Pilot Officer Andrew McLure in the process. His aircraft will fly again.

Unlike Hurricane P3222 of 238 Squadron from RAF Middle Wallop. It was shot down off Weymouth by a Messerschmitt Bf109, killing Pilot Officer Frederick Norman Cawse. He was aged 22

A Messerschmitt Bf110 fighter-bomber was accounted for by Pilot Officer Noel le Chevalier Agazarian of 609 Squadron from RAF Warmwell.

12 August   **Heinkel shot down at Sturminster Marshall.**

A Heinkel He111 (1G+AC), heading homeward via Dorset's Stour valley after a raid on Bristol docks, was intercepted at 02.00 hours today by a British night-fighter. The bomber was raked with cannon fire and the pilot, who has been identified as a "Gruppenkommander", parachuted to captivity along with his four crewmen.

Their aircraft crashed in flames at Sturminster Marshall. Its "1G" markings indicate it belonged to Kampfgeschwader 27, a bomber wing.

13 August   **Warmwell Spitfires have five Dorset kills.**

Eagle Day: the Luftwaffe's Adlertag attack of nearly three hundred aircraft against military targets in central southern Engrand has been routed. At noon a Messerschmitt Bf110 (L1+FZ) crashed in flames at Swalland Farm, Kimmeridge. "L1" shows it belonged to Lehrgeschwader 1, a unit formed to test new aircraft of all types, and innovate tactics, under operational conditions. The two crew baled out and were taken prisoner.

Warmwell's Spitfires were scrambled at 15.30 hours. "Achtung, Achtung, Spit und Hurri", Pilot Officer David Moore Crook, flying R6699 (PR-L), heard repeatedly as he approached the German formations. One of the 27 Junkers Ju87 "Stuka" dive-bombers of II Gruppe Stukageschwader 2 that had been targeted on Middle Wallop Airfield, Hampshire, was shot down between Portesham and Rodden at 16.00 hours, killing its two crewmen, Feldwebel Linderschmid and Gefreiter Eisold. The kill was claimed by Flight Lieutenant Derek Boitel-Gill of 152 Squadron. At the same time Pilot Officer Crook of 609 Squadron sent a Messerschmitt Bf109 smoking into the cloud and descended to see the debris of a crash near the Hardy Monument. This, however, was that of another enemy aircraft, which came down two hundred yards from the railway station at Grimstone, killing both crew. They were Feldwebel Erich Haach of Krossen, and Gefreiter Henrich Myer, or Meir, from Oberhausen. The two crew and the discovery of an unexploded 250-kilogram bomb in the wreckage confirm that it was a "Stuka" or a Bf110 fighter-bomber.

None of the enemy aircraft deployed today reached its target.

As for the Messerschmitt Bf109 E1 escort fighters being chased by 609 Squadron, as they turned for the coast short of fuel, Crook's kill ended up in Poole Harbour. The pilot, Unteroffizier Wilhelm Hohenseldt, was rescued and made a prisoner of war. Another Bf109 was shot down into the sea off Weymouth. Its pilot, Leutnant Heinz Pfannschmidt, was also saved and taken prisoner. This kill was claimed by Pilot Officer Tadeusz Nowierski, who is avenging the rape of Poland.

The Hurricanes of 238 Squadron, from RAF Middle Wallop, also took part in the dog-fights but two were lost in the process. One of the pilots, Sergeant Pilot Ronald Little, was driven away unhurt after P3805 had crashed at Bredy Farm, a mile east of Burton Bradstock.

There were few lucky Germans, but the day's most fortunate Briton was Flying Officer John Dundas of 609 Squadron from Warmwell. His Spitfire, N3113, narrowly pulled clear from collision with a "Stuka" and in the process he found his oil system ruptured by a bullet from its gunner. His propeller stopped. Dundas skilfully used his height, from off Portland, to glide down to a successful forced-landing at Warmwell Aerodrome.

Footnote Eyewitness E.G. Read of Stratton recalled the Grimstone crash for me in 1981: "My neighbours and I had been watching an aerial battle and machine gun ammunition clips had fluttered down around us. Suddenly there was a bloodcurdling banshee wail. It was heart-stopping as it approached us.

"Right over our heads came the stricken plane [from the north-east]. There was dense black smoke pouring from its starboard engine [the

"Stuka" was single-engined, so if remembered correctly this indicates a Bf110] and the two young airmen were clearly visible. They had just seconds to live. Later came the news that a German plane had crashed behind Grimstone viaduct. We went there immediately on our bikes, but a sentry was there on guard with fixed bayonet. Beneath two white parachutes were the crumpled bodies of the airmen.

"The next day the sentry was gone and we went souvenir hunting. I pulled off a small electrical bakelite plug that was stamped 'Made in England'. The two young fliers were interred in a green unploughed curve at the side of a field. Later two ornately carved and inscribed wooden crosses appeared at the spot. The bodies remained there from that sunny afternoon in 1940 until the late 1960s when they were reburied at the Brookwood military cemetery, Surrey.

"I found their crosses in a dilapidated shed at Frampton churchyard in 1964. The galvanised roof was holed and they were covered in wet lichen. Since then both shed and crosses have disappeared. So, too, has my souvenir component, which I inadvertently threw out with an unwanted box of oddments before moving house in 1978."

13 August   **An entry in the Dorchester Observer Corps log.**

Time: 16.35 hours, Location: Poundbury Camp [north-west of the county town of Dorchester]. Area of activity: South of sector R4, Dorchester. Report: "Confirmed hostile and friendly pilots approaching the post. Much machine gun and cannon fire. Fierce contest going on. Plane shot down believed Bf110, another plane down, much confused sound-plotting and heavy firing for a considerable period. One plane believed friendly, flying low east. Believed forced landing this side of the Maiden Castle House and in neighbourhood of the Fever Hospital."

Footnote John Norman of the Royal Observer Corps remembered that emergency Spitfire touch-down for me in 1980: "It landed in the field at Maiden Castle Farm at the back of the cottages and I cycled over in time to see it take off."

14 August   **Second transatlantic crossing from Poole.**

The Air Ministry Under-Secretary, Harold Balfour, is flying today from Poole to the United States on the second wartime transatlantic flying-boat crossing by *Clare*.

Footnote The flying-boat was back in Poole on the 18th. Balfour bought three Boeing 314s — "Clipper" flying-boats — from the Americans. These long-range boats will be delivered to British Overseas Airways at Poole early next year.

15 August   **Kills for 152 Squadron and Spitfire pilot swims home.**

Nine Spitfires of 152 Squadron, from Warmwell Aerodrome, were at 15,000 feet above Portland at 17.15 hours when they heard over the radio: "Many enemy aircraft approaching Portland from the south."

Two minutes later a cloud of black specks became visible in mid-Channel, at about the same height as the British fighters. There were an estimated one hundred or more enemy aircraft, with Junkers Ju87s in tight V-formations each comprising three "Stukas" surrounded by Messerschmitt Bf110 escorts.

The Spitfires climbed to 18,000 feet in a wide circle that brought them out of the sun to descend through the German ranks about five miles south of Portland Bill. The resulting mêlée, which was joined by Hurricanes from Exeter, had a mixed outcome.

Ralph "Bob" Wolton of 152 Squadron was shot down in the engagement with the "Stukas" and fell out of his Spitfire seconds before it crashed into the sea. He managed to swim to one of the offshore marker buoys of the Chesil Beach bombing range, from which he was rescued by an RAF launch from Lyme Regis.

Pilot Officer Harold John Akroyd, also of 152 Squadron, limped home to Warmwell with a jammed rudder, following an engagement off Portland in which he accounted for a Junkers Ju87. Sergeant Pilot Denis Robinson shot down a Bf110.

Flight-Lieutenant Frank Howell of 609 Squadron returned to Warmwell with the claim of a Junkers Ju88 kill.

15 August   **A pilot dies a hero at Abbotsbury.**

Twenty-seven-year-old Squadron Leader Terence Lovell-Gregg of 87 Squadron, from Exeter, failed in a desperate attempt to make a crash landing in The Fleet lagoon late this afternoon. The Hurricane came in blazing from over the sea but was brought into a controlled descent for a forced landing. P3215 then clipped a tree beside Abbotsbury Swannery and its wounded pilot fell to his death.

Flying Officer Roland Prosper Beamont, one of the Exeter pilots, returned with the story of how Lovell-Gregg had led his squadron into the midst of a mass of German aircraft at 18,000 feet over the English Channel: "We saw the 'Beehive' almost straight ahead at the same height, and with his Hurricanes, Lovell-Gregg flew straight at the centre of the formation without hesitation or deviation in any way."

One hundred and twenty enemy aircraft were heading towards Portland. Lovell-Gregg was a quiet pre-war professional, from Marlborough in New Zealand, who had taught many of the emergent generation of flyers. His courage was never in any doubt, though he had led his squadron for only a month, since 12 July. The pilots knew him as "Shovel". There were only four of them with him when they scrambled at 16.00 hours today. Five Hurricanes were all the air-worthy machines that 87 Squadron could muster. Undaunted by the adverse odds of fifteen-to-one that loomed in front, Lovell-Gregg asked the impossible of his men: "Come on chaps, let's surround them!"

Two of the other Hurricanes were also crippled but their pilots lived. P3465 crash-landed at Symondsbury, near Bridport, and R2687 was forced down at Field Barn Farm, beside the marshland of Radipole Lake at Weymouth.

Footnote William Dunford, then an Abbotsbury schoolboy, described for me how he put out the flames on the Squadron Leader's burning body. "Lovell-Gregg's Hurricane was shot down in flames, at about 6 to 6.30 pm, but he recovered control to put the plane into a perfect glide and attempted to land in The Fleet lagoon at Abbotsbury Swannery. He came low over a small wood but was not quite high enough. The underside of the Hurricane hit the top of an oak tree, and Lovell-Gregg was thrown out of the cockpit. The plane went on through the trees and crashed.

"With another schoolboy I ran to the spot where the pilot had fallen. He was badly shot about and burning. We put out the flames with two buckets of water. About two hours later a truck came from Warmwell and we were then told the flier's identity. Though he had those wounds, I am sure, had he made it into the water, that he would have survived." Lovell-Gregg is buried in Warmwell churchyard.

Ironically, in St Nicholas's Church at Abbotsbury there is a plaque recording with thanks that no one from the parish died on active service or from enemy action in the Second World War — without any mention of their heroic defender from the other side of the world.

15 August   Spitfire crashes at Bournemouth.

The eastern side of the Middle Wallop Sector also saw action today with a formation of bombers approaching Bournemouth. The Spitfires of 234 Squadron were scrambled from RAF Middle Wallop at 17.05 hours and intercepted the bombers, which were heading homeward, over the town. A sustained air battle took place at 4,000 feet, during which Spitfire R6988 was hit by fire from one of the German rear gunners.

It spiralled into Leven Avenue, to the west of Meyrick Park golf links, leaving a crater and wreckage across a wide area. One of the wings fell on a hedge in Walsford Road. Pilot Officer Cecil Hight fell from the aircraft but his parachute did not open. The New Zealander had been seriously wounded and apparently passed out before he could pull the rip-cord. His body was found in Mr and Mrs Hoare's garden; his stomach had been ripped open by machine-gun bullets.

Footnote The town has named Pilot Hight Road in his memory. Cecil Hight was the only allied airman to die over Bournemouth during the Battle of Britain. He is buried in Boscombe Cemetary and a memorial tablet was unveiled at St Peter's Church in the town centre on 7 April 1943.

Mr and Mrs Hoare's house was again to be visited by the war. Ian McQueen records in Bournemouth St Peter's that it was hit by a German bomb. Canon Hedley Burrows recalled that it was the house where Hight's Spitfire had crashed.

"The dear old man, Mr Hoare died," Canon Burrows said, but then they heard Mrs Hoare.

"Who is that?" she asked. "I am Canon Burrows; keep still; they are going to get you out."

"Canon Burrows," she repied, "how kind of you to come and see me today."

16 August **152 Squadron's Beaumont has a double.**

Pilot Officer Walter Beaumont, flying a Spitfire with 152 Squadron from Warmwell Aerodrome, has scored his squadron's first double kills with two Messerschmitt Bf109s brought down over the Isle of Wight at lunchtime.

In the evening, as the second patrol of the day was about to head for home, two Heinkel He111s were spotted below, at 3,000 feet over the Solent. The rear one was attacked at 18.15 hours by Pilot Officer Eric Simcox Marrs. "Boy" is his nickname; he is aged nineteen but looks much younger.

As the Heinkel came out of a bank of mist he shot it up: "I left it with smoke coming from both engines and my own machine covered in oil from it. I don't think it could have got home and I'm pretty sure it didn't."

His claim is not being accepted, because a radio transmission was misunderstood, and no one else in the squadron had seen the action. Marrs, however, is in no doubt, and he is writing to his father: "I am counting that as my first."

17 August **Warmwell's Robinson claims a 'Stuka'.**

Sergeant Pilot Denis Robinson of 152 Squadron returned to RAF Warmwell from today's sweep over the English Channel with the claim of a Junkers Ju87 "Stuka" successfully intercepted and shot down into the sea.

18 August **Warmwell's 'Boy' Marrs as his first confirmed kill.**

Formations of more than a hundred "Stuka" dive-bombers, escorted by Messerschmitt Bf109 fighters, crossed the Channel to attack the radar station at Poling and aerodromes at Ford, Thorney Island and Gosport. Eleven Spitfires of 152 Squadron were scrambled from Warmwell.

The Spitfires dived from 4,000 feet on the "Stukas" as they swept back to sea after dropping their bombs. Pilot Officer Eric "Boy" Marrs claimed a kill, his first that would be confirmed:

"We dived after them and they went down to about a hundred feet above the water. Then followed a running chase out to sea. The evasive action they took was to throttle back and do steep turns to right and left so that we would not be able to follow them and would overshoot. There were, however, so many of them that if one was shaken off the tail of one there was always another to sit on. I fired at about six and shot down one. It caught fire in the port wing petrol tank and then went into the sea about three hundred yards further on."

The "Stukas" were from I and II Gruppen of Stukageschwader 77, the same unit as Von Dalwigk's dive-bomber, shot down on 9 July. They suffered sixteen losses as 43, 601 and 602 Squadrons joined 152 Squadron in the action. The Bf109 escort fighters were routed by the Spitfires of 234 Squadron from RAF Middle Wallop.

18 August **Marrs goes 'Tally-ho' again.**

17.25 hours. On his second combat patrol of the day, Eric "Boy" Marrs of 152 Squadron from Warmwell Aerodrome has led the three Spitfires of

Blue Section in a "Tally-ho" after a German Dornier Do17 which was flying towards Portland.

The interception took place from 16,000 feet and the bomber dropped into cloud at about 5,000 feet. Marrs has emptied his guns and the third Spitfire is claiming a share in the kill.

Footnote Apparently it was not that decisive and the bomber managed to return to France.

19 August   'Enigma' decrypt gives warning of Warmwell attack.

01.52 hours. "From a reliable source, information has been received of an impending attack on Warmwell aerodrome this morning. Aircraft are to be ready to leave at 07.00 hours." [The source being a German "Enigma" radio signal decoded by the Government Code and Cipher School, at Bletchley Park, Buckinghamshire].

21 August   Two killed by afternoon bombs at Poole.

Mrs Pauline Fairbrother of 38 Market Street and Frederick Landrey of 18 South Road were killed this afternoon when a single German raider, a Junkers Ju88, came in low over the Old Town area of central Poole from Sandbanks. It dropped six bombs.   The one that killed Mr Landrey destroyed the National School air-raid shelter, thankfully unoccupied, and the others hit shops and timber stores.

23 August   Two killed by Lulworth raider.

A lone German raider attacked Lulworth Camp today a few minutes after the "All Clear" had sounded. Recruits had resumed their infantry training and were in the open as the aircraft approached. Sergeant J. Thompson shouted to them to get down and stay still.

Eight bombs were dropped on the sportsfield, the ranges and at St Andrew's Farm which is inside the camp complex. Two men were killed and seven injured, the latter including Sergeant Thompson who received severe leg wounds. He had been in the stores when he heard the aircraft approaching and but for his instant and brave response, when he put himself into the line of fire to warn the men, there would have been a greater number of casualties.

23 August   24 killed by bombs at New Milton.

Twenty-four people were klled and many injured this evening when Junkers Ju88 bombers devastated Station Road, New Milton. The seaside village's main street has flats above the shops and is surrounded by a residential area.

Air Raid Precautions units, ambulances, and fire engines are in attendance from Christchurch and Lymington. Train services into Dorset have been temporarily diverted from Brockenhurst to Poole, northwards via Ringwood and Wimborne, but it seems that the railway track is probably undamaged.

25 August **Shops bombed at Poole.**

Early this morning a single German bomber attacked the Ashley Road and Constitution Hill area of Upper Parkstone, Poole, destroying three shops and a house. Two people were injured.

25 August **Decoded signals rouse Warmwell to action-packed day.**

07.40 hours. "It is reliably reported that air attacks are to be expected during the course of today 25th August 1940 at Warmwell, Little Rissington and Abingdon aerodromes and reconnaissances by a single aircraft in the area Southampton-Aldershot-Brighton." [The intelligence source being German "Enigma" machine-coded radio signals deciphered by the Government Code and Cipher School at Bletchley Park.]

By 17.00 the twelve Warmwell Spitfires of 152 Squadron were airborne. Half an hour later the station was rocked by twenty bombs, which destroyed the sick quarters and damaged hangars. Delayed action bombs went off over the next couple of days. The Spitfires had met Luftflotte 3 over Portland but despite the advance warning it was a more or less even match.

Hurricanes of 213 Squadron joined in the dog-fights from Exeter. They lost two fighters and a third, N2646, crash-landed at Burton Bradstock but is repairable and the pilot, Sergeant Pilot Ernest Snowden, unhurt.

Sergeant Pilot Sidney Richard Ernest Wakeling of Exeter's 87 Squadron, aged 21, was killed when his Hurricane, V7250, plunged in flames at New Barn, on the hillside south of Bradford Peverell, near Dorchester.

There are also a number of German crashes. A Messerschmitt Bf109 has crashed on the Chesil Beach at Chickerell and its pilot, Hauptmann Maculan, apparently fell out and drowned. A Bf110 has exploded at Tatton House, between Langton Herring and Buckland Ripers, killing both crew. A Bf109 came down in an adjoining field on Tatton Farm and its pilot escaped with wounds as it was engulfed in flames. He was taken prisoner.

Shortly after 18.00 hours, a Bf110 was reported crashing at Creech Barrow, the conical shaped summit in the Purbeck Hills south of Wareham, and another Bf110 (3M+KH) came down at Priory Farm, East Holme. Both sets of crew parachuted into captivity. A third Bf110 (3M+CH) was taken on by two 609 Squadron Spitfires, those of Squadron Leader H.S. "George" Darley and American volunteer Pilot Officer Eugene Quimby "Red" Tobin, and put down at East Chaldon, to west of Lulworth. It became a fireball and the crew died in the explosion. "3M" indicates that both aircraft belonged to the 1st Staffel of II Gruppe, Zerstörergeschwader 2.

This Sunday evening, to balance those kills, there is a report that two of 609 Squdron's Spitfires have not returned to RAF Warmwell. Both pilots have survived, though one is wounded. 152 Squadron has also lost two Spitfires, over the sea, but their news is bleaker and Pilot Officers Richard Malzard Hogg and Timothy Seddon Wildblood have been posted "Missing in Action".

Squadron Leader Darley, the commanding officer of 609 Squadron, accounted for the first Messerschmitt to be brought down. In all, the squadron claims eleven, and certainly several Bf110 fighter-bombers from ll Gruppe ZG/2 and V Gruppe ZG/1 were destroyed, and Bf109 fighters from II Gruppe Jagdgeschwader 2, a fighter wing named Richthefen, though these escorts had succeeded in keeping the Spitfires from the Junkers Ju88 bombers.

Of the Germans on the ground, one has been identified. It was Gefreiter Josef Bröker's Bf109 of JG/53 that belly-landed by a wood at Tatton Farm, Buckland Ripers, to the north of Chickerell. The credit is claimed by Pilot Officer Walter Beaumont of 152 Squadron who has driven out from Warmwell and arrived "in shirtsleeves and sweat" at the scorched scene of his triumph.

Bröker has been taken prisoner of war and will survive his burns.

27 August   152's Beaumont bales out off Portland.

Pilot Officer Walter Beaumont was able to bale out of Spitfire R6831, belonging to 152 Squadron from RAF Warmwell, as it was hit by return fire from a Junkers Ju88. His fighter crashed into the sea about eight miles off Portland.

Beaumont, who survives to fight another day, had just shared the honours in the destruction of a Heinkel He111 bomber.

29 August   Extensive bomb damage at Poole.

04.00 hours. Though no one has been injured, high explosive and incendiary bombs have caused considerable damage to buildings in the Longfleet, Oakdale and Parkstone suburbs of Poole.

29 August   Bombs miss Christchurch.

Early this morning incendiary bombs landed near the Priory, Millhams Street and at Queens Avenue in Christchurch, One was on the roof of the air-compressing station. There were also the thuds of high explosive bombs but daylight revealed they had dropped on the north side of the town into heathland and woods at St Catherine's Hill. Ten had gone off and one had failed to explode.

August   Burton Bradstock call for Hitler prayers.

Writing in *The Two Edged Sword*, Adela Curtis, leader of the Christian Contemplatives' Community at St Bride's Farm, Burton Bradstock, advises on methods of furthering the war effort through positive prayer: "We are to summon each enemy leader by name. For cumulative effect the message should be spoken three times – Adolf Hitler! Adolf Hitler! Adolf Hitler! Hear the Truth!"

August   Cranborne Chase motor-cycle exercises.

The 4th Battalion of the Royal Northumberland Fusiliers have been reorganised as a motorcycle reconnaissance column and are based at Blandford Camp. Their sidecar patrols are seemingly everywhere in the Cranborne Chase villages.

The 2nd and 8th Battalions of the Fusiliers are also in Dorset, dispersed through the Blackmore Vale.

4 September   **Another Warmwell pilot killed.**

Sergeant Pilot John Barker, in a Spitfire of 152 Squadron, was killed in action today. He scrambled from RAF Warmwell for an operational sortie.

Sergeant Pilot Denis Robinson returned with the claim of a Junkers Ju88 destroyed.

5 September   **Bomb hits Druitt's House, Christchurch.**

Druitt's House, the solicitors' offices and former residence of one of the town's leading families – which produced Montagu John Druitt who was a suspect for Jack the Ripper, the Whitechapel murderer – was destroyed by a German bomb at 01.30 hours this morning. Just after midnight a bomb had dropped on Iford golf course but that one failed to explode.

7 September   **Spitfire crashes near Dorchester.**

Ralph "Bob" Wolton, flying at the rear of a flight of Spitfires with 152 Squadron from Warmwell, today lost control of his fighter whilst attempting a sudden dive. He jumped from the falling plane at 13,000 feet though he estimates that it was not until nearly a thousand feet from the ground when he managed to sort out the cords and activate the chute. The Spitfire crashed near Dorchester.

No enemy plane was involved.

Flight-Lieutenant Frank Howell of 609 Squadron returned to RAF Warmwell with the claim of a Messerschmitt Bf110 that he had shot down.

7 September   **The great invasion scare.**

The German invasion appears to have started. Reports have been received of a seven-mile convoy heading towards the Dorset coast and there is a general flap on that Operation Sealion is taking place and Field-Marshal Fedor von Bock is on his way with the victors of Poland, the Wehrmacht's Army Group B. The fuel tanks are to be fired to set the beaches ablaze and an aircraft from Gosport is dropping incendiaries to start them off.

Troops at Bournemouth have manned the cliffs and keep emphasising that this is not an exercise.

The Home Guard at the Supermarine aircraft factory in Southampton has been alerted to enemy landings at Portsmouth.

7 September   **Invasion expected tonight.**

20.07 hours. A national alert has been issued by the War Office: "Condition Cromwell". An invasion is regarded as imminent and probable within twelve hours.

Footnote Nothing happened! One set of "Fougasse" tanks ignited a beach but the plane was recalled to Gosport before it set alight to any more. There was no landing in Dorset or anywhere else. Despite that, invasion fears had reached fever-pitch and not only in the popular imagination, for aerial reconnaissances were showing concentrations of ships and barges in harbours from Brest to Calais.

10 September   **Fourteen bombs at Christchurch.**

Fourteen bombs landed in the Christchurch area last night, at about midnight, fracturing water mains and bringing down telephone wires. There was serious blast damage to Hoburne Farm.
    Six of the bombs fortunately exploded harmlessly on Chewton Common.

13 September   **609's Howell has his fourth kill.**

Flight-Lieutenant Frank Howell of 609 Squadron at RAF Warmwell has claimed his fourth kill, that of a Junkers Ju87 "Stuka" dive-bomber.

14 September   **Warmwell loses a further pilot.**

A further fatal casualty has been inflicted upon RAF Warmwell, taking the life of Flying Officer C.O. Hinks.

15 September   **Warmwell's Spitfires defend London.**

The Spitfires of 609 Squadron from Warmwell were drawn into the air defence of London today as the Battle of Britain reached its climax. Total claims for the day were 186 enemy aircraft shot down. Among them were a Dornier Do17 bomber shot down by Flight-Lieutenant Frank Howell and a half-share in another Dornier, claimed by Pilot Officer "Red" Tobin.

    Footnote The Air Ministry was warned by its own intelligence department that "kill" claims were being overstated and that no more than 76 planes could have been destroyed on 15 September. Post-war examination of German records showed that even this was exaggerated; the real figure was 62.
    For all that it was a victory. Air Chief Marshal Sir Hugh Dowding had handled his forces with precision and economy. They had not been wasted on pointless patrols. A combination of radar and decoded German radio traffic meant that the sectors that were going to have a quiet day – as with Middle Wallop and Warmwell on the 15th – could provide planes for an area where the resident defenders would be outnumbered. Dowding's achievement was to deny the Luftwaffe its one prerequisite for winning the Battle of Britain. This was done by ensuring there were always planes in reserve and that something could be done about the following day's attack.
    Göring was frustrated by this and had ordered his commanders: "You must bring the RAF up to battle."

15 September   **Cattistock carillon destroyed by fire.**

14.30 hours. The tall 1873-built tower of Cattistock parish church has been gutted by fire, destroying its famous carillon of thirty-five bells. The village will miss the tunes. Officially the cause is not known, but locally it has been blamed on a cigarette discarded by a member of the Home Guard who was in the tower for fire-watching.

15 September   **Heinkels turn back from Portland Bill.**

Intercepted by B Flight of six Spitfires of 152 Squadron from RAF Warmwell, led by Pilot Officer Eric "Boy" Marrs, thirty Heinkel He111 bombers dropped their bombs from 16,000 feet over Portland Bill and turned back towards France.

The Spitfires harried them for ten miles, claiming to have shot down two and damaged others. Marrs writes: "If we had had the whole squadron up we could have broken their formation and knocked down quite a number. The extraordinary part about this raid was that there was no fighter escort."

One Heinkel He111, probably belonging to Kampfgruppe 55 from Chartres, was definitely destroyed.

The three Spitfires of Green Section each had a turn with five-second bursts of cannon fire. Pilot Officer Peter O'Brien, in Green One, attacked the starboard engine from astern. Sergeant Pilot Kenneth Holland, in Green Three, followed from astern and above, reporting black smoke pouring from the starboard engine. Then Pilot Officer Weston, in Green Two, delivered the coup de grâce at 15.55 hours.

17 September   **Marrs gets a Junkers but loses his 'Old Faithful'.**

Pilot Officer Eric "Boy" Marrs was leading Blue Section of 152 Squadron from RAF Warmwell over Portland earlier this afternoon. He was then told to rise to 20,000 feet on a course of 350 degrees, which eight minutes later was changed to 280 degrees. This brought him in sight of a lone Junkers Ju88 bomber (L1+XC) above Shepton Mallet, Somerset. It belonged to operational test unit Lehrgeschwader 1.

"Tally-ho" Marrs called over the radio from Blue One, as he led the three Spitfires in line astern. The first burst from his guns hit the radiator of the bomber's starboard engine and had it streaming with white ethylene glycol coolant. The bomber descended into thick cloud, heading east, and would crash-land at Ladywell Barn, two miles west of Imber, Wiltshire, only three miles from Dauntsey's which was Marrs's old school.

Marrs, however, then suffered engine failure. "Old Faithful", in which the young pilot had flown 130 hours was coaxed down from 12,000 feet on to the concrete runways of a disused aerodrome at Yatesbury that's partly obstructed to prevent German landings.

A bullet had smashed the air cooler and caused the Merlin engine to lose its oil. A maintenance squad removed the Spitfire by road and Marrs will never fly it again; probably it will go back into service with a training unit.

Sergeant Pilot Kenneth Holland, in Blue Two, also, sustained damage from the Junkers, to hydraulic, glycol, and oil pipes, and came down at Yatesbury as well, puncturing his starboard tyre. He had been hit by machine-gun fire in three places; and had himself pumped 1,650 rounds in the general direction of the Junkers.

Only one Spitfire, Blue Three flown by Pilot Officer Peter O'Brien, was able to return directly to Dorset and Warmwell Aerodrome.

The Ju88 was from the Luftwaffe base at Bricy, near Orleans, and its crew was headed by Major Cramer, Gruppe Kommandeur of LG1. He and two others would survive the crash-landing. The fourth man was killed.

They had been on their way towards factories at Speke, near Liverpool. Each Spitfire pilot personally claimed one-third of the kill.

17 September   **Operation Sealion postponed indefinitely.**

Hitler today postponed Operation Seelöwe [Sealion], the planned invasion of England, which should give the country's nerves a reprieve until next spring. Winston Churchill has read out a deciphered German Enigma machine-coded radio message to the Chiefs of Defence Staff — a minor order of huge significance, for the dismantling of loading equipment on Dutch airfields. Churchill refers to Sealion as Operation Smith, to lessen the risk of compromising the Enigma intercepts that revealed its name.

19 September   **Bournemouth Garrison stood down.**

With the abandonment of Operation Sealion any immediate prospect of a German invasion has receded and accordingly the Bournemouth Garrison has stood down. The Garrison Commander has been replaced by a new posting, that of Officer Commanding Troops, Bournemouth.

19 September   **Warmwell's Holland claims a Junkers.**

Green Section of 152 Squadron scrambled this afternoon from RAF Warmwell and ordered to patrol the cloud base at 10,000 feet. They found that Spitfire Green One's radio telephone was unserviceable, so Green Two — flown by Sergeant Pilot Kenneth Holland took over and became Green One.

Holland was told to climb to 15,000 feet above Warmwell Aerodrome and vectored towards a Junkers Ju88 bomber. His combat report begins at 16.20 hours:

"As there was cloud at 10,000 feet, Green Two went below the cloud and I went above the cloud at 11,500 feet. When cloud broke I went down to given height and sighted Ju88 ahead on the right two miles away. Green Two was left behind below cloud.

"I gave 'Tally-ho' on the R/T [radio telephone] but Green Two could not find me.

"I made alternate quarter attacks from left and right, from 300 to 200-yards, firing one burst of four-seconds and – five each of two-seconds, aiming first at gunners' positions and then at each engine.

"E/A [Enemy aircraft] took slight evasive action, heading for cloud on a southerly course. White return fire after my second attack.

"I continued to attack and eventually the E/A, now at 8,000 feet, dived vertically towards the sea, with both engines on fire. As my ammunition was finished I flew on a northerly course, and came to the Isle of Wight.

"My engine was missing slightly so I made for Portsmouth Aerodrome where I landed. After checking engine returned to base. Rounds fired — 2,800."

20 September   **Steamship sinks in Lyme Bay.**

SS *Trito*, a British steam freighter, has sunk after being bombed by German aircraft in Lyme Bay.

23 September   **Warmwell loses another pilot.**

Pilot Officer Walter Beaumont, flying Spitfire R7016 of 152 Squadron from RAF Warmwell, is believed to have been shot down over the sea. He has been reported as "Missing in Action".

Beaumont enlisted in the Royal Air Force in December 1939 and would claim 152 Squadron's first double set of kills, over the Isle of Wight on 16 August. It was regarded as tempting fate when he drove to visit the wreckage of another of his successes on 25 August.

24 September   **Six killed as Navy trawler hits mine.**

His-Majesty's Trawler *Loch Monteith*, on an anti-invasion patrol in Lyme Bay, hit what is presumed to have been a mine at 02.45 hours this morning. The bows are severely damaged and six men were killed as they slept.

Her location is ten miles west of Portland Bill and she is being towed back to Portland by the dockyard tug *Pilot*.

25 September   **Heinkels shot down at Poole and Studland.**

A German mass bombing force of 220 attacking planes and their escorts passed over Portland and flew to the Bristol Channel coast where they turned between the islands Steep Holm and Flat Holm and made an approach across the water towards the Bristol Aeroplane Company's works at Filton. This was devastated by 350 bombs and from 15,000 feet the aerodrome rippled with flashes.

On the way home, however, the raiders were harried by the RAF. Five aircraft were brought down and a further three had to crash-land in France. The two shot down in Dorset were both claimed by Hurricanes of 238 Squadron from Middle Wallop. One Heinkel 111 (markings G1+LR) ploughed into "Underwood", a house at Westminster Road, Branksome Park, and all but one of its five crewmen were killed.

The second Heinkel 111 (G1+BH) crash-landed at Westfield Farm, Studland. Josef Attrichter, the flight mechanic, was taken from the wreckage but died half an hour later. The other four crewmen had aching backs from the impact but survived. Wine waiter Theo Janku took them prisoner with the aid of an unloaded Home Guard rifle and relieved them of their Lugers. On seeing there were casualties the Studland villagers then tried to help the Germans and provided cigarettes and tea.

"G1" identifies the Heinkels as belonging to Kampfgeschwader 55, their emblem being the coat of arms of Giessen.

Footnote Later the second Heinkel was salvaged and reassembled for Cardiff's war weapons week. Before it was removed from Studland it had been guarded by a detachment of the Suffolk Regiment. "This is war, not a bloody peepshow," one of the sentries snapped at onlookers. It seems to have been from this bomber that a document was found forbidding the use of explosive ammunition against troop concentrations and other human targets.

The burial of the Branksome Park Germans in Parkstone Cemetery, next to graves of British seamen, enraged the Poole Herald which protested that "Nazi murderers and British heroes" were "placed side by side" and a week later felt utterly let down by one of its readers: "Someone has put flowers on the grave!"

| 25 September | **Warmwell pilot killed in Somerset.** |

Another of today's Heinkel kills, that of Hauptmann Helmut Brandt's He111 (G1+EP) belonging to II Staffel of Kampfgruppe 55, is being credited to a Spitfire of 152 Squadron from RAF Warmwell.

The wreckage of both aeroplanes is strewn across fields at Church Farm, Woolverton, a village four miles north of Frome, Somerset. The crash sites are less than 500 yards apart and occurred within minutes of each other.

Sergeant Pilot Kenneth Christopher Holland hit the ground first, at noon precisely. He died almost immediately from the effects of the crash and a severe bullet wound to the head, which had apparently caused him to lose control of the fighter.

Then at 12.02 the German bomber came down. The pilot had baled out and survived but the other three crewmen were killed, one in the fireball on impact, and the others from having jumped at a height too low for their parachutes to function.

Twenty-year-old Kenneth Holland also used the surname Ripley. He was an Australian orphan, from Manley in Sydney, who came to England to enlist in the RAF, joining 152 Squadron at Warmwell on 1 August.

Squadron Leader Peter Devitt of 152 Squadron also had problems with a Heinkel He111, which ruptured the petrol tank of his Spitfire with a burst of return fire. Devitt made a successful forced-landing in the Avon valley between Bristol and Bath, at Skew Bridge, Newton St Loe.

| 26 September | **More Warmwell and German losses.** |

Flight-Lieutenant Derek Boitel-Gill led a section of 152 Squadron from Warmwell into combat against a formation of Junkers Ju88s and their Messerschmitt Bf109 escort fighters over the sea to the west of the Isle of Wight. One was seen to fall into the water, the kill being the work of Ralph "Bob" Wolton. Two of the Spitfires were lost in the combat, however, with Sergeant Pilot Jack McBean Christie being reported "Killed in Action" and

Flying-Officer "Jumbo" Deansley bailing out of K9982. He was picked-up by an RAF Air-Sea Rescue launch and landed at Swanage.

Some sixty Heinkel He111s of Kampfgeschwader 55 have wrecked the Vickers Supermarine works at Woolston, Southampton — the main centre for Spitfire production — with seventy tons of bombs. More than thirty people have been killed.

Footnote Boitel-Gill was no mean shot, having been credited with five kills in a week in August. He became Commanding Officer of 152 Squadron early in 1941 and Wing Commander in June. He then lost his life in a flying accident, in July 1941.

27 September   **Marrs puts his Junkers down in the Bristol Channel.**

Pilot Officer Eric "Boy" Marrs from 152 Squadron, flying a Warmwell Spitfire, started what was going to be an active day by finding a lone Junkers Ju88 at 23,000 feet over Somerset. He followed it in a running fight across Exmoor, flying at only fifty feet in places, and had ethylene glycol coolant streaming from both engines of the bomber.

The German pilot headed for the coast, but by a different channel from that over which the Dorset Spitfires usually patrol: "As I expected both engines soon stopped. He made for the south coast of the Bristol Channel and landed about twenty feet from the beach in the water, running his machine up on to the beach. I circled round and watched the crew get out. They waved to me and I waved back, and then hordes of civilians came rushing up. I watched the crew taken prisoner, beat up the beach, and then climbed away."

The tiny seaside resort treated to this excitement was Porlock, west of Minehead. It is unusual for anything to happen here, the village's single claim to fame being "a person on business from Porlock" who interrupted Samuel Taylor Coleridge as he was recalling and writing down his dream-poem *Kubla Khan* and who remains unknown to this day.

27 September   **Lulworth AA gunners get a Bf110.**

Anti-aircraft gunners at Lulworth Camp are jubilantly celebrating their first definite kill. The unlucky German aircraft was a Messerschmitt Bf110 which had come low over the huts. There had been an air raid warning and a red alert was in force. The stricken fighter crashed to ground about a thousand yards from the sea.

27 September   **German planes crash all over Dorset.**

This Friday has been the day when German planes crashed all over Dorset, plus Mick Miller and his Spitfire from 609 Squadron. The full account of the abortive raid on the Parnell Aircraft Company – makers of gun turrets – at Yate, near Chipping Sodbury, was told in 1979 by Kenneth Wakefield in his *Luftwaffe Encore*.

Ten fighter-bombers of Erprobungsgruppe 210, an experimental and proving unit from Cherbourg, led by Hauptmann Martin Lutz, had the support of 89 fighters. The Gruppe's aircraft have as their crest a red map of the British Isles superimposed with a yellow ring-type gun sight. They were testing bomb-carrying on Messerschmitt Bf109s and Bf110s.

The German bombers, coming in fast over north Bristol on their attacking run at 11,000 feet, were met head on by Murray Frisby in a Hurricane. He scored a hit that damaged Lutz's plane, and the others too were forced to turn. The rest of 504 Squadron, scrambled from Filton, chased after the scattering planes and forced them to jettison their bombs. Escape was now the only German objective.

One of the Bf110s was shot down over Fishponds, Bristol. Another came down at Haydon Hill, near Radstock.

That was 11.45 in the morning. At the same moment, over Bellamy's Farm, Piddletrenthide, there was a similar bang as one of the rearguard manoeuvres went wrong. Pilot Officer Mick Miller, in Spitfire X4107 and leading 609 (West Riding) Squadron — scrambled from Warmwell, where they arrived each morning from Middle Wallop — had collided with a Bf110 (number 3U+FT) at 24,000 feet. Miller and the Messerschmitt's wireless operator, Emil Lidtke, were killed instantly. But the German pilot, Georg lackstedt, was able to free himself and parachuted (minus his boots) into a field. He was given some lemonade and then taken off by police.

His dead comrade was treated with less respect: "Ralph Wightman recalled hat when the body was removed from the wreckage it was left in full view for some hours before someone covered it with a sheet. Later a dispute arose over the burial, one report indicating that the local clergy refused to bury the body; apparently the dead airman was eventually buried beside the hedgerow where he fell." That was the boundary between Bellamy's and Dole's Ash Farm. The Spitfire came down to the east, nearer Cheselbourne. Miller was an Australian.

Another Bf110 (3U+IM) was exploding at about 11.45, at 1,000 feet over Salter's Wood, Middlebere, in Purbeck. It had been attacked by a Spitfire of 152 Squadron, Warmwell's second squadron. In the crashed plane were Arthur Niebuhr and Klaus Deissen. Both were killed.

Equally unfortunate, at 11.50, were the crew of another Bfll0, between Tyneham and Kimmeridge. It was almost certainly aircraft 3U+BD manned by Hans Carschel and Unteroffizier Klose. Luckier — five-minutes later and only a mile away — were the crew of 3U+DS. Fritz Schupp and Karl Nechwatal had been attacked by Spitfires and their port engine was hit and burning. But Schupp successfully brought his plane to a crash landing near Gaulter Gap. It had three 'kill' bars, which as Wakefield says, denoted "victories over RAF aircraft". The "3U" aircraft were from Zerstörergeschwader 26, the Geschwader named Horst Wessel, after the Nazi writer of a militant anti-semitic song which became a national anthem.

At noon, another Bf110 (S9+DU) made a belly landing. It received engine damage over Iwerne Minster and came down at The Beeches, beside the A350. The pilot was Friedrich Ebner, who was unhurt, but the gunner, Werner Zwick, was taken to Shaftesbury Hospital with major wounds.

Another noon crash was at Bussey Stool Farrn, near Tarrant Gunville. It was S9+DH – the Bf110 of the attack's leader, Martin Lutz. It had been damaged at Bristol. The plane was travelling at speed but losing height and hit trees before ploughing into the ground. Both Lutz and his radio operator, Anton Schön, were killed. Lutz was aged 27, and had flown with the Condor Legion in the Spanish Civil War.

Two Bf110s were also shot down at mid-day into the sea off Dorset. One was S9+JH, the crew being Gerhard Schmidt and Gerhard Richeter, whose bodies were later recovered. The crew of the other plane, S9+GK (Wilhelm Rössiger and Hans Marx) were never found. They were brought down 25 miles south of Portland Bill. The attacking Spitfire was flown by Noel le Chevalier Agazarian, from Warmwell. The "S9" aircraft belonged to Erprobungsgruppe 210.

27 September   Agazarian's three kills for 609 Squadron.

Warmwell's Armenian-French Spitfire flyer, Pilot Officer Noel le Chevalier Agazarian of 609 Squadron, has scored a hat-trick of kills over the past three days. His previous claim was a month ago with a shared Messerschmitt Bf110 on 25 August.

The current run of good fortune began with another shared kill, that of a Heinkel He111 bomber, on 25 September. That was followed by an exclusive Messerschmitt Bf109 fighter yesterday, and today an unshared but confirmed Bf110 fighter-bomber — put down in the sea — which has been identified as S9+GK.

Footnote Agazarian was killed later in the war but he left one of the most evocative of all memorials. His fighter, R6915, survived the war and is now suspended over the displays in the Imperial War Museum, Lambeth Road, London SE1. It dominates the exhibits, as does Dorset's Roman mosaic of Christ in the British Museum.

28 September   Navy trawler sunk by mine.

An underwater explosion heard off Portland at 21.16 hours last night is believed to have sunk His Majesty's Trawler *Recoil*, which is as the *Blankenburg* was captured from the Germans.

The explosion was heard from her sister vessel, HMS *Angle*, which went to the spot to investigate. Though no wreckage was found there was a stench of diesel oil in the vicinity. It coincided with *Recoil's* last known position.

29 September   Christchurch radar establishment hit.

01.07 hours. Six high explosive bombs and a number of incendiaries dropped on to the Ministry of Supply's Air Defence Experimental Establishment which makes radar components at Somerford, Christchurch. Damage, however, is slight. All the fires were put out by 02.48.

30 September   Morning and afternoon claims by Crook of Warmwell.

Scrambling at 11.00 hours from Warmwell Aerodrome, in Spitfire X4165, Pilot Officer David Moore Crook led Green Section of 609 Squadron as they swept in a line seawards across the Isle of Purbeck. Pilot Officer Mike

Appleby quickly put a Messerschmitt Bf109 into the sea, but Crook's action was protracted.

He records the sortie in his log: "We intercepted some Bf109s at 23,000 feet over Swanage. The fools tried to escape by diving and we all went down after them. I got up to about 300 mph and easily caught mine, gave it a burst and he crashed into the sea. I then chased another and put him into the sea about twenty-five miles from Cherbourg. It took me a long time to get back to the English coast . . . pleased to see the white cliffs."

Crook was airborne again in the afternoon, leading Green Section in combat against six Bf109s, ten miles north of Poole: "I had a very enjoyable few minutes dog-fighting with one and though behind him all the time could not get sights properly on him. Finally he dived for cloud, but I chased him to Weymouth and then gave him a good burst. He turned over to his back and spun into cloud streaming glycol and smoke. I could not claim him as definite as I did not see him actually crash but he certainly never got back to France. This was my best day yet."

Footnote David Crook was awarded the Distinguished Flying Cross on 17 October 1940.

His last operation with 609 Squadron, leading it in the Commanding Officer's absence, would be on 8 November 1940, also in Spitfire X4165. He became a flying instructor. Norman Franks records Crook's fate in the book *Wings of Freedom*. On 18 December 1944, at the age of thirty, he was lost over the North Sea, off Aberdeen, whilst flying Spitfire EN662 on a high-level photographic reconnaissance. He left a widow, Dorothy, and a four-year-old son, Nicholas.

30 September   **Sherborne's 60 bombs in a few minutes.**

Yeovil's barrage balloons were raised a few minutes before four o'clock on a warm but cloudy afternoon. In Sherborne the air-raid sirens also wailed.

Thirty-seven Heinkel He111 bombers were attempting to find the Westland Aircraft Company's factory in Yeovil but precision was impossible due to nine-tenths cloud cover at 20,000 feet.

Instead, flying information on a line north-north-east they missed their target by five miles and began to bomb blind in the vicinity of Lenthay Common and then across the ancient yellow-stone town of Sherborne, raining about sixty bombs down on to its clustered terraces and between scholastic and ecclesiastical roofs.

Townspeople insist that the raid was over in a matter of minutes. Remarkably, the town's famous Abbey and other historic buildings are almost unscathed, and casualties are light considering the extensive overall damage to shops, homes and roads. Fortunately the schools had just gone home.

Seventeen are dead and there are 32 hospital cases, one of whom is critically injured.

Footnote The badly injured person would die. Theirs was to be just about Sherborne's only direct sacrifice for the duration of hostilities; only four others went to hospital as a result of the war in the period 1939-45 . Despite the damage, in a line across the town from Lenthay Common to

Coldharbour, it was of little architectural consequence. The Abbey, Sherborne School, the Almshouse, Sherborne Castle and even the older ruined castle survived with only flecks of superficial damage. For all that it was by far the worst air attack of the war on one of Dorset's inland towns.

There was a heroine amongst the debris. Miss Maud Steele, the supervisor of the telephone exchange which was blown apart by a direct hit, stayed calm and ensured that the town's initial calamity reports were sent out by road.

She was to be awarded the George Cross for her pluck; it had been instituted by King George VI as the "Civilians VC" only a few days previously. The town had 766 damaged buildings, some ten per-cent of them devastated, out of a total of 1,700. The sewers as well as the phones were out of action. Blankets had to be brought in by the Red Cross and a council appeal fund, competing with many others, raised £2,200 including contributions from Sherborne in Massachusetts.

For the victims there is a brass plate behind the cross that commemorates the Great War in Half Moon Street, in front of the Abbey precinct:

THOSE WHO DIED IN THE AIR RAID ON SHERBORNE
30 SEPTEMBER 1940

BUTLIN John	LE GALLAIS Albert I.E.
DAWE Leonard I.	LINTERN Arthur J.
GARTELL Albertina B.	MARDEN Elizabeth A.
GOULTER Percy H.D.	MORGAN William S.
HUNT Douglas	REASON A.H.
IRELAND Henry	TRASK Barry A.
JEFFERY William C.	WARREN Ronald K.
KNOBBS Edward D.	WARREN Robert G.
LEGG Horace G.	WARREN Patricia A.

In 1984, for the story of the disaster and the town's resilience and recovery, I interviewed the District Air Raid Precautions Controller, Edward J. Freeman MBE who was also the Clerk to the Sherborne Urban District Council between 1936-74. The account was first published in Harold Osment's *Wartime Sherborne*. In it Mr Osment poignantly recalls that one of the dead was a schoolchum: "There came the cruel realisation, so cruel as to be almost beautiful, that we should never again see, let alone play with Bobby Warren." This is how Mr Freeman recalled the day and its aftermath, from his bungalow beside the fields at Rimpton, to the north of the town:

"The Sherborne raid is being forgotten. Last year I heard a guide at Sherborne Castle say in answer to a question, about whether any bombs had fallen at Sherborne during the war, that he thought there had been one dropped in the town. I interrupted to say that I had been the town's ARP Controller and there had been 300 bombs [60, actually] that fell in three minutes on 30 September 1940.

"At the time I was on the pavement in Yeovil standing in a queue to see a picture – it was one of the few days in the entire war when I was away from my desk. It was my birthday. The thud of the bombs in the east was followed by a pall of black smoke, which could only be from Sherborne, and I drove straight back. It took me twenty minutes to reach the council offices, picking my way through an unimaginable shambles.

"The theory is that the fifty German planes had been on their way to the Bristol Aeroplane. Company works at Filton" [seriously damaged by an attack five days earlier, on 25 September, though in fact the attack was against Westlands at Yeovil] "and were intercepted by a squadron of Hurricanes, two of which were brought down each side of Yeovil. The local people thought one of the pilots was a German as they saw his parachute open. The bombers came to us from the south-west, across Lenthay Common, and then they unloaded. We were underneath.

"There were no longer any services at all. No water, no telephones — the exchange had a direct hit — no gas, no electricity, and the sewers and all roads out of the town were blocked.

"One of the miracles was in Newland where Foster's Infants School received a direct hit and had to be pulled down afterwards. It was hit only a quarter of an hour after the children had left. One story I heard, though I cannot vouch for it, was that in The Avenue Miss Billinger climbed from her bath into the open air. Perhaps the strangest damage was in Horsecastles where bombs landed on both sides of the terrace and the outhouses imploded away from the main buildings, which was caused by a bellows effect. Six or eight delayed action bombs went off twelve hours later. One caught us out as it was hidden under debris. The strangest debris came from the midnight bakery next to the Picture Palace in Newland. They had hoarded silver coins which were thrown on to the cinema roof and retrieved by my ARP warden.

"As I plotted the bombs on to our ARP area map and the number climbed into the hundreds I ran out of red pins. It was quite extraordinary that there hadn't been more casualties.

"The worst thing was a direct hit in the cemetery. The coffin of a friend whom we had buried a week earlier was blown out of the ground. My gravediggers disappeared and we did the best we could to clear up with a firm of undertakers from Yeovil.

"Down Lenthay there was terrible damage and I sent the Billeting Officer down on his bike to see how many I had to rehouse and find accommodation for. Ten of our council houses were completely destroyed, and there was damage to all the remaining 108 of them, mainly on a serious scale. To my astonishment when he came back he said, 'No need to worry — people have come forward and offered shelter. Everyone has been given a home somewhere.' It was quite extraordinary what happened there, and it happened all over the town. If ever I have admired the people of Sherborne as a whole it was after the raid.

"I had told the schools they might have to put people up that night, but in the event it wasn't necessary. One little thing, after that raid there was no all-clear as we had no electricity. From then on we had to use rattles and a whistle for air raid sirens.

"The ministry men thought I was exaggerating and panicking when they heard from me on the only emergency phone line we had left, but when they came down they apologised to me. They had never seen such complete devastation in a small country town.

"I took the Regional Commissioner around in my car. Twelve hours later all my tyres were flat, punctured by the glass.

"Opposite Phillips and Son's store, outside the Westminster Bank, an unexploded bomb had fallen, leaving a hole that the bomb disposal team had covered with sandbags. An officer calmly sat down beside these on a lump of stone and lit a cigarette. I showed some concern that we were sitting down beside a bomb. 'If it goes off, we won't know anything about it,he said.

"'It's a big one' he said, 'but I can't touch it for a fortnight. In the meantime you'll have to evacuate everyone around.' The police and army sealed off the area and we got the stretcher cases out as best we could.

"I had to arrange temporary rationing arrangements because we couldn't get into the butcher's shop.

"A fortnight later that officer came back to me laughing, saying: 'You'll never believe this, Mr Freeman, but it was only a small one. The big hole was because it had gone down a disused well shaft!'

"I was flooded with visits from people in London, Bristol, Reading and the cities, and had to explain how we got out of difficulties. It is surprising how the help came that we needed, there was a wonderful spirit everywhere.

"The ministry admitted there were certain things we had to do that might be outside the law, but they said go ahead anyway as legislation was on the way.

"I still wonder how the devil we coped with it all. Twenty or thirty evacuees would come down the day after a London raid and we would have to find homes for them. The evacuation was worked out on paper and by the train timetables, but we would have cases where 600 would come down from one school, bound for Sherborne, and some of ours would get off at Sidmouth. We had to sort that out, have the doctors inspect them, and give out 48-hours rations. You saw how people had been living in London. It was a trying time, particularly as my staff were being called up. We coped by making our minds up at a moment's notice.

"One night I had a red warning that there would be a raid, and suddenly the whole place was lit up by parachute flares, but then nothing happened. We had been told that if the flares dropped they would be followed by bombs. The lights ringed the town and someone phoned to say there was a landmine hanging out of his front door, but it was a flare that had caught in his chimney. He was so excited and frightened he said he couldn't get out of the house — I asked him what had happened to the back door!

"I kept on good terms with most of the town. The only time I upset the school was when I requisitioned its tuck shop as a British Restaurant.

"Later in the war, because of our experiences, we were chosen for bomb instruction exercises, and a special invasion exercise in Newland in May 1943. For that one they had a particularly realistic casualty, with his eye hanging by a thread, provided by the butcher. I think they went too far. One old lady in the crowd fainted.

"My biggest regret is that I didn't keep a diary, but I never had the time. A little regret is that there was a relic of the raid that could have been preserved, three pieces of bomb-case that were embedded out of harm's way in a school wall. I asked General Waller, the bursar, to leave them but he had them hooked out and the stone repaired."

30 September   **The 'Boy' who just made it back to Warmwell.**

The Heinkel He111s that jettisoned their bombs on Sherborne had been met by 152 Squadron as they flew at 21,000 feet over Portland. They had apparently been intending to raid Filton, at Bristol, or the Westland Aircraft factory at Yeovil which makes the Whirlwind, though with only a hundred produced this is set to turn into a failure. Anyway, the bombers were heading northward.

Squadron Leader Peter Devitt could only muster eight Spitfires of 152 Squadron at RAF Warmwell "and some of these should not have flown by peacetime standards". He was ordered by Sector Control to proceed as quickly as possible to Yeovil. Devitt found it covered with cloud and there was no sign of the enemy:

"Thinking that perhaps they had delivered their bombs and swung round through 180 degrees to starboard, as they had done on a previous Bristol raid, I turned the squadron eastwards in the hopes of picking them up. They had obviously turned this way so as not to be silhouetted against a background of white cloud for our fighters to pick up. It is always more difficult ti pick up a camouflaged aircraft from above and with the earth below, but a fighter must have the advantage of height in order to deliver his full weight in the first attack.

"A few seconds after I had spotted them I saw their bombs falling away from beneath their bellies. On looking down to see what the target was, to my horror I saw the old school courts which I knew so well." Devitt was at Sherborne School from 1924 to 1929.

"I was at that time just in a position to attack which I did, but was molested by a pack of Bf109s which I had not noticed sitting above the Heinkels, and above me as well. I could not see much of where the bombs fell as I was too intent on what was going on around me. I did, however, see in one instant a great deal of smoke around the old buildings and so knew there must be some hits and damage and probably casualties."

After his engagement with the formation that was to cause havoc in the abbey town of Sherborne, 19-year-old Eric' "Boy" Marrs (so called from his engagingly youthful looks) limped back to Warmwell in a crippled Spitfire and found that only one of his wheels would come down. It would not then retract, and to attempt a landing on one wheel is much more hazardous than a belly flop. He turned off the engine and glided in to land, touching down on the grass as gently as possible: "I began to slew round and counteracted as much as possible with the brake on the wheel which was down. I ended up going sideways on one wheel, a tail wheel and a wing tip. Luckily the good tyre held out and the only damage to the aeroplane, apart from that done by the bullets, is a wing tip which is easily replaceable.

"I hopped out and went to the MO to get a lot of metal splinters picked out of my leg and wrist. I felt jolly glad to be down on the ground without having caught fire."

Warmwell has, however, had a loss today. Sergeant Pilot Leslie Arthur Edwin Reddington went down in the sea with Spitfire L1072 of 152 Squadron. He came from Coventry and was aged 26.

56 Squadron, from RAF Boscombe Down, has had half its Hurricanes put out of action over Dorset today, though without any casualties among the pilots. Hurricane P2866 crashed at East Knighton, near Wool, and N2434 was shot down over Okeford Fitzpaine. Both pilots parachuted safely. Pilot Officer Maxwell crash-landed Hurricane L1764 on the pebbles of the Chesil Beach across the water from Abbotsbury Swannery. Hurricanes P3870 and P2910 force-landed, though without major damage, at Warmwell.

A Bf109 flown by Unteroffizier Alois Dollinger of 5/JG 2 Richthofen was shot down over Hundred Acre Farm, Sydling St Nicholas. Its pilot baled out but was found dead. His Black 2 had flown from Le Havre/Octeville.

Footnote The Sydling crash site would later be farmed by escaped British prisoner of war and author George Millar, who wrote *Maquis* [1945], *Horned Pigeon* [1946] and *Through the Unicorn Gates* [1950]. This was the longest range of all the Bf109 crashes of 1940.

For the month as a whole, September 1940, Warmwell's 609 Squadron claimed nineteen German aircraft for the loss of two Spitfires. Even allowing for overclaiming, the result was decisive. The confusion over claims was inevitable in that often several fighters had a part in accounting for the same bomber and it was frequently impossible to follow victims down to the ground. Station morale would have been depressed by continual inquests over dubious claims. What dropped on to the fields showed the trend, but the sea could anonymously accommodate any amount of further hopes.

30 September   **Hurricanes join the exhilarating coastal combat.**

Perhaps the most exhilarating flying of the day was enjoyed by 238 Squadron, flying Hurricanes from RAF Middle Wallop. Flight-Lieutenant Michael Lister Robinson, in R4099 (VK-S), led the nine fighters south over Poole Bay and turned at Swanage to head towards Portland.

They climbed into the cloud at 5,000 feet and rose to 15,000 feet above St Alban's Head, on a gyro-compass course westwards to get the advantage of the setting sun in Lyme Bay before wheeling into a dive on the German formations that were heading towards Portland.

They saw the enemy 3,000 feet below, to port, and swung into head-on attack. Robinson engaged a Messerschmitt Bf110 from 300 yards, ripping it to pieces and sending an aerial oil-slick across his cockpit, which cleared sufficiently to give him a view of the Messerschmitt splashing down some ten miles south of Portland Bill.

Still with a smeared windscreen, he then saw another Bf110, which was at 7,000 feet and heading back to France. Robinson gave chase and came to within a hundred yards before opening up with three seconds of fire that pulled the port engine apart and moments later had the Messerschmitt explode. Its remains fell upside-down into the English Channel, fifteen miles south of Portland Bill.

Robinson then flew north, towards Portland, and climbed to 25,000 feet to join a line of what he thought were Spitfires, but which turned out to be Bf109s. He still continued towards them and took on the closest, giving it a sustained six seconds of fire from 300 yards. Debris, smoke and white glycol streamed out as it flipped over and dropped seawards.

Mike Robinson switched to his gravity tank: "Landed at Exeter, no petrol." It was 16.30 hours; he heard that others in 238 Squadron also had something to celebrate, including Pilot Officer Bob Doe who had shot down a Heinkel.

Robinson and Doe joined the squadron only two days ago.

September   **Blockship barrier to Weymouth Harbour.**

The veteran cargo steamer *Kenfig Pool*, which has been moored beside Hope Quay in Weymouth Harbour since July is being placed across the harbour entrance at nights and prepared for scuttling. She is to act as a barrier in the event of the anticipated German invasion.

September   **'Beams' scientists dispersed to Langton Matravers.**

The Telecommunications Research Establishment at Worth Matravers has requisitioned Leeson House and Durnford School in the nearby village of Langton Matravers. Further expansion of its hutted encampment beside Renscombe Farm, on the west side of Worth, had been considered inadvisable. The tall aerials of the coastal radar research station are already attracting the attention of German bombers.

Scientists at Worth and Langton are deeply involved in what has become the "Battle of the Beams". The Luftwaffe is targeting inland English objectives by an intersection of radio pulses – one of synchronised dots and the other of dashes – transmitted from Kleve, in Germany, near the Dutch border south-east of Arnhem, and from Stolberg near the Danish border.

Dr Robert Cockburn has developed a Radio Counter Measure which is codenamed "Aspirin". This duplicates the continuous morse dashes, which are being transmitted on a frequency of 30 to 31.5 megacycles per second, and disorientates the German pilots by widening their direction beam.

A more ambitious plan was, in effect, to bend the beam by recording a sequence of synchronous German dots and re-transmitting the signal from a mast at Beacon Hill, near Salisbury. This scheme was thwarted, however, because the telephone land-line that Dr Cockburn was using, from Worth Matravers to Beacon Hill, was taken over by the military.

The signal was recorded in the Isle of Purbeck but without the telephone link it could not be re-radiated from Beacon Hill.

Asynchronous signals are, however, having the desired effect without more sophisticated forms of interference being necessary.

1 October   **Plane crashes off Hengistbury Head.**

An unidentified aeroplane fell into the sea off Hengistbury Head, Bournemouth, at 10.55 am. Machine gun fire had been heard. No one baled out.

2 October   **609 Squadron now exclusively at Warmwell.**

Much to the relief of the pilots, the Mark I Spitfires of 609 Squadron are no longer flying their daily shuttle from RAF Middle Wallop, on the Hampshire Downs, to Warmwell Aerodrome in south Dorset.

From today they cease to be day visitors and are now based at RAF Warmwell.

7 October   **Four die as bomb blasts Weymouth bus depot.**

Four died and many were injured when the Southern National bus depot at Weymouth received a direct hit by a German bomb. Fourteen buses and coaches were badly damaged.

7 October   **More Warmwell kills and losses.**

609 and 152 Squadrons from RAF Warmwell clashed with German aircraft on their doorstep, at times over the aerodrome itself, as an enemy force crossed the Channel at Portland to bomb the Westland Aircraft factory at Yeovil where a hundred civilian workers have been killed in a direct hit on an air-raid shelter. Four kills were credited to 609 Squadron but for the loss of two Warmwell Spitfires with critical injuries to Pilot Officer Harold John Akroyd and the death of Sergeant Pilot Alan Norman Feary.

Akroyd, who is aged 27, received crippling damage to his fighter over west Dorset. Spitfire N3039 burst into flames on crashing at Nutmead, Shillingstone. Though he was pulled clear of the wreckage he is suffering extensive burns.

Feary was hit by Messerschmitt Bf109s over Weymouth. He baled out from Spitfire N3238 as it crashed at Watercombe Farm, between Warmwell and Owermoigne, but was too low for the parachute to open.

Pilot Officer Eric "Boy" Marrs, in Spitfire R6968, led Blue Section of 152 Squadron at 20,000 feet over the eastern Frome valley. They descended upon fifty German Junkers Ju88s and Messerschmitt Bf110s with Bf109 escorts.

The enemy fighters were weaving defensive circles behind the bombers. Marrs waited for the final Bf109 to pull out of a ring, in order to catch up with the bombers, and then struck at the last Bf110 fighter-bomber in the exposed line. It belonged to II or III Gruppe of Zerstöregeschwader 26 and had the nose section painted white.

As glycol coolant streamed from the Messerschmitt's starboard engine, Marrs switched his fire leftward across the fuselage: "Suddenly the back half of his cockpit flew off and out jumped two men. Their parachutes streamed and opened and they began drifting slowly earth-wards. Their aeroplane, left to itself, dived vertically into the sea, making a most wonderful sight and an enormous splash . . . everything seemed to have cleared off, so I circled round the two Huns. They took an awful long time to come down on land and I watched the army rush up to capture them."

Footnote Akroyd died of his burns the following day. The two RAF officers are buried in the RAF plot at Warmwell churchyard. "ONE OF THE FEW" Feary's stone reads. He was aged 28.

7 October   Close call for Spitfire R6915 and John Dundas.

Engaging a defensive ring of fifteen Bf110s, above Cheselbourne and Dewlish at 16.30 hours, Flight-Lieutenant John Dundas, leading Blue Flight of 609 Squadron from RAF Warmwell, flew guns blazing over the top of the Messerschmitts. Then as he climbed away from the circle of fighter-bombers he came across a lone Bf110 at 16,000 feet.

Approaching its tail he gave a sustained twelve seconds of fire from his eight guns. Both engines belched smoke and white ethylene glycol coolant.

As John Dundas closed again on his crippled target its gunner hit back with a shell that splintered his leg and sent Spitfire R6915 reeling into a spin. Pilot and aircraft both recovered sufficiently to level out and glide into Warmwell Aerodrome.

The burning Me110 was spotted crossing the coast at Weymouth, at 14,000 feet, and is presumed to have crashed in the English Channel, though Dundas will only have credit for a probable kill. Flight-Lieutenant Frank Howell has also claimed the kill of a Bf110.

Footnote Spitfire R6915 is the machine that now hangs from the ceiling of the Imperial War Museum as its main Battle of Britain exhibit. It has already been mentioned, on 30 September 1940, when its flyer was Noel le Chevalier Agazarian. As for John Dundas, he was back in the air next day, and awarded the Distinguished Flying Cross on 10 October. He reappears in the story on 27 and 28 November.

7 October   German aircraft shot down at Lulworth and Owermoigne.

15.45 hours: a formation of German aircraft, estimated in excess of sixty, are approaching the coast at Lulworth.

15.50: the attackers are engaged by the anti-aircraft gunners at Lulworth Camp and by Warmwell's Spitfires which are intercepting them as they cross the Frome valley.

15.55: meeting heavy opposition the German aircraft have turned back towards the sea.

16.37: the air raid sirens have given the All Clear at Lulworth where a Messerschmitt Bf110 was seen to fall into the sea about 2,000 yards off the Arish Mell Gap. Another German aeroplane is understood to have crashed close to Owermoigne.

7 October   Hurricane crashes at Alton Pancras.

56 Squadron, flying Hurricanes from RAF Boscombe Down, Wiltshire, joined in today's hectic air activity over Dorset and Yeovil. A detachment was sent to Warmwell Aerodrome and were scrambled at 16.00 hours.

They met an estimated fifty Messerschmitt Bf110 fighters over Bulbarrow Hill in central Dorset. Hurricane P3154 was shot down in flames from 25,000 feet above Alton Pancras. Sergeant Pilot Dennis Hugh

Nichols, aged nineteen and on his first combat mission, was able to parachute clear of the stricken fighter but landed badly and has been taken to Dorchester Hospital with a suspected fracture of the spine.

Footnote Nichols would be in hospital for months and did not resume operational flying until 1942. He survived the war and enjoyed an active retirement, returning to Alton Pancras to see relics of P3154 being excavated from the crash-site in 1994.

8 October **Warmwell pilot dies after Shillingstone crash.**

Pilot Officer Harold John Akroyd of 152 Squadron from RAF Warmwell has died from burns received yesterday when his crippled Spitfire, N3039, burst into flames on crashing at Nutmead, Shillingstone. It had been crippled by enemy fire in the dog-fights over west Dorset.
He was aged 27, and will be buried in the RAF plot at Warmwell churchyard.

8 October **Bomb wrecks Moreton church.**

21.00 hours. Moreton's eighteenth century parish church has been completely wrecked by a German bomb that fell beside the north wall. This has collapsed and the glass is blown out and destroyed. The building is a ruin.

Footnote St Nicholas's Church was restored and re-dedicated, in May 1950, and since 1955 has been enriched by the finest set of modern engraved glass windows in Britain – the creation of Laurence Whistler.

10 October **Hurricane pilot killed at Wareham.**

Czechoslovakian flyer Sergeant Pilot Jaroslav Hlavác of 56 Squadron, from RAF Boscombe Down, was killed at 12.20 this afternoon when Hurricane P3421 was shot down at Manor Farm, Worgret, to the west of Wareham. He was aged 26, had been with the squadron just two days, and was in the process of intercepting a flight of Messerschmitt Bf109s. The body is being taken to Warmwell churchyard for burial in the RAF plot.
Hurricane P3984 of 238 Squadron, from the newly opened RAF Chilbolton, Hampshire, crashed at 13.00 hours below Corfe Castle — missing the famous ruin by only 200 yards and plummeting into a roadside quarry just north of the Castle Hill. It came down close to the viaduct that carries the railway across the Studland road.
This time the pilot, though wounded, was able to bale out. Pilot Officer Bob Doe landed on Brownsea Island and has been taken to Cornelia Hospital at Poole. He is twenty years old and was recently awarded the Distinguished Flying Cross.
The lunchtime problem for the Hurricanes seems to have been the dense cloud-base which extended up to 16,000 feet. As British fighters came up through it they were visible to the enemy formations in the clear sky above – but for those last fatal moments the visibility for the RAF pilots was still obscured by water droplets.

11 October   **Poole boy killed by bomb.**

Stanley Ricketts, an 11-year-old Poole boy, was fatally injured this evening by a German bomb as he walked home at Kingsbere Road. Incendiaries also landed in the Constitution Hill area and other parts of the town, including the Cornelia Hospital where Stanley died.

14 October   **Lyme minefield claims another Navy trawler.**

The British armed trawler HMT *Lord Stamp* has sunk after striking a mine in Lyme Bay.

15 October   **609 Squadron get a Bf110 over Bournemouth.**

Leading Blue Flight of 609 Squadron from Warmwell Aerodrome, in Spitfire P9503, Flight Lieutenant John Dundas flew through the gunfire of three Messerschmitt Bf109 fighters at 14,000 feet over Christchurch. One Spitfire reported a bullet hole, but no apparent damage, though the squadron's flight pattern was thrown into disarray.

Dundas failed to regroup his flight and soared alone to 18,000 feet where he found some fifteen Bf110 fighter-bombers. He made two runs at them, giving bursts of fire from only a hundred yards, but then broke away as Bf109s came on the Spitfire from above.

An Bf110 has reportedly crashed near Bournemouth as a result of the engagement. It is the squadron's ninety-ninth accepted kill.

16 October   **Bovington and Poole air-raids.**

Cryptanalysts at Bletchley Park, deciphering the German "Enigma" radio traffic, gave warning of today's bombing raid on east Dorset, which hit Bovington and Poole. The intercepted signal was "Target No. 1 for Y".

Target No. 1 is known to be the Armoured Fighting Vehicles School at Bovington, and "Y" indicates that Y-beam radio direction signals were being used. The Y-Gerat target finding system is deployed by the pathfinding 3rd Gruppe of Kampfgeschwader 26 (whose aircraft carry the identification marking "H" to the left of the iron cross on their rear fuselage).

17 October   **Further Navy trawler goes down.**

The Royal Navy's losses of armed trawlers to the German minefield off west Dorset continued today when HMT *Kingston Cairngorm* blew up off Portland Bill.

17 October   **The 'false invasion'.**

An intended raid on the Dorset and Devon coast to cover the infiltration of fifth columnists, mostly Irish Republicans, has been thwarted by the Royal Navy. Submarine L27, an ex-Danish boat, has shadowed the attack on the German convoy and many of the enemy have drowned, including SS agents. It has been the day of the false invasion.

The German force included the 5th T-boat Flotilla, 1,300-ton motor torpedo boats the size of a light destroyer, and the destroyers *Karl Galster*, *Friedrich Ihrs*, *Hans Lody* and *Erich Steinbrinck*. They are having a running fight to escape from a mixed Allied force of two British cruisers supported by two Free French destroyers, two Norwegian destroyers, and one each from the Dutch and Danish navies.

18 October   **Warmwell pilot killed at Tadnoll Mill.**

Sergeant Pilot Edmund Eric Shepperd, flying Spitfire R6607 of 152 Squadron from RAF Warmwell, was killed today when his fighter plunged into the ground. No other aeroplane was involved and there was no obvious reason for the accident.

It happened at Tadnoll Mill, two miles south-east of Warmwell Aerodrome, in the northern extremity of Chaldon Herring parish.

19 October   **Bournemouth firemen go to London.**

Bournemouth firemen, who were the first provincial reinforcements to arrive in the capital at the beginning of the Blitz in September, among the fifty pumps at Millwall Docks, have now instigated an exchange scheme with London firemen. Forty members of the Auxiliary Fire Service, from Bournemouth – divisional area 16C of No.6 Region – will today swap duties for a week with some of the city's exhausted heroes.

Deputy Chief Officer Ken Devereux is leading the Bournemouth team and it is expected that they will gain valuable experience in tackling major bomb damage.

Footnote   Ted Hughes, who dealt with the administration at the Bournemouth Fire Service headquarters, records in *Bournemouth Firemen at War* that 625 of his men attended city blitzes in Southampton, Portsmouth, Bristol, Exeter and Plymouth as well as London, and that on 83 occasions they drove their pumps to the action. Usually that was at night, with only much diminished cowled slit-lights, along roads without any direction signs.

19 October   **Two 12-inch guns en route for Dorset.**

Two 12-inch Mark II railway-mounted howitzers, dating from the Great War, have been released, to Southern Command from the Ordnance Depot at Chilwell, Nottingham. They have arrived at Ringwood where they will remain in a siding until they can be deployed in the Isle of Purbeck.

21 October   **Two share 609 Squadron's hundredth kill.**

Pilot Officer Sydney Jenkyn Hill and Flight-Lieutenant Frank Howell today share the credit for the destruction of a Junkers Ju88 bomber and returned to RAF Warmwell in jubilation. This kill is 609 Squadron's hundredth victory.

Aged 23, Hill is Dorset-born, from Ferndown, near Wimborne. Howell is a Londoner, from Golders Green.

Footnote   Sydney Hill would be killed by Messerschmitt Bf109s, on 18 June 1941, and is buried in Folkestone New Cemetery, Kent.

Frank Howell was awarded the Distinguished Flying Cross on 25 October 1940. Posted to RAF Filton, where he formed 118 Squadron on 20 February 1941, he later moved to the Far East where he was captured by the Japanese after the sinking of the battleship HMS *Prince of Wales*, on 10 December 1941.

Post-war, Squadron Leader Howell lost his life in a bizarre aerodrome accident, being decapitated by the wing of a Vampire as he was filming his jets with a cine-camera, on 9 May 1948.

22 October   **Portland minefield sinks the 'Hickory'.**

The *Hickory*, a diesel-powered civilian vessel, is the latest victim of the German minefield off Portland.

26 October   **Bournemouth's Carlton Hotel becomes Rations Office.**

The prestigious Carlton Hotel on the East Cliff at Bournemouth has been requisitioned by the Board of Trade for use as a ration-coupon issuing office for the documents that are now needed for the restricted allowances of petrol and clothes.

In recent months the new Rations Office has only had five residents, since visitors were banned from the Defence Area, and one of these, Mrs Myers, has been fined 10 shillings with £1 12s 6d costs for an infringement of the blackout. The hotel felt obliged to pay.

October   **Pilot Officer Pooch is Warmwell's mascot.**

Pooch, the mascot of 152 Squadron at Warmwell Aerodrome, is reputed to have sired most of the bull terriers that are in RAF service.
He carries the honorary rank of Pilot Officer and generally guards 152's dispersal hut. This is adorned with a collection of signs "lifted and borrowed" by Spitfire pilots from the farms and countryside around Weymouth and Dorchester.

"JOE GUPPY'S CAMP" — the sign above the door, from Preston — is unlikely to be needed for the duration of the conflict. The losers of "SAFETY FIRST: BEWARE CATTLE" and similar miscellaneous road signs can take solace from the fact that their messages of carefulness and courtesy are being absorbed by impresionable young minds.

October   **31,000 acres of Dorset grasslands ploughed for corn.**

Grain production for Dorset might have been a record in any case, given the hot summer, but it is way beyond anything in living memory as a result of 31,000 acres of pasture being hastily turned over to arable food production. The familiar greens of downland sheep walks and the dairying vales way to golden expanses of wheat and barley.

More ephemeral, exotic even, were drab dusky fields that suddenly turned into splashes of vivid cyan blue as the sky brightened. This crop is flax, the flowers of which open only for the sun.

T.R. Ferris, executive officer of the Dorset War Agricultural Committee, has announced next year's target: "The committee has been given a task of ploughing out of grass a further 22,000 acres of land for the 1941 harvest." Most of this land will be sown with grain but he is also appealing to gardeners and allotment holders "to do their utmost to increase food production by growing vegetables in all parts of the county".

October   **Dorset's Somaliland hero returns from the dead to a VC.**

Captain Eric Wilson of Long Crichel, who was seconded to the Somaliland Camel Corps, has been gazetted posthumously for the victoria Cross as a result of his part in the heroic defence of the.British colony in the Horn of Africa during the Italian invasion of 4-19 August. He commanded a series of Bren gun positions that were blown to pieces in a sustained attack over four days and he held out until the end.

The award was cited in the London Gazette but the story does not end there as three days later news reached the British that Captain Wilson had survived and was prisoner-of-war.

Footnote Neither would the story end there. As the war turned against the Italians he was liberated and fought with the Long Range Desert Group. Lieutenant Colonel Wilson retired from the Army in 1949 and became an administrator in Tanganyika, until 1961, before returning to a West Country cottage, at Stowell near Sherborne.

October   **Winterbourne Abbas loses last church band.**

The last church band in England is now a memory as William Dunford, its sole surviving player, has taken his bass-viol home from Winterbourne Abbas parish church.

October   **Bournemouth's Home Guard totals 8,000.**

Recruitment of civilian volunteers into the Hampshire Regiment (Home Guard) units under the control of the Officer Commanding Troops, Bournemouth – whose area includes the other two towns in the conurbation, Poole and Christchurch – is set to reach eight thousand men. The detachments and their approximate manpower on call, nominally, at least, are:

3rd (Poole) Battalion – 2,500 men
6th (Bournemouth) Battalion – 2,300 men
7th (Boscombe) Battalion – 2,500 men
22nd (Post Office) Battalion – 400 men
B Company (Southern Railway) Battalion – 300 men

October   **City pets evacuated to Shaftesbury.**

The animal shelter opened by Nina, Duchess of Hamilton, on her estate at Ferne to the east of Shaftesbury has become a refuge for hundreds of city pets, made homeless by the bombings and the general upheavals of war. As far as possible they are being cared for as if they were still at home, with freedom and exercise, rather than being permanently impounded in cages. Larger animals, such as horses, ponies and goats, are also being given refuge.

  In reply to criticism that it is a waste of resources to care for animals in wartime, the Duchess quotes a Regional Commissioner of the Ministry of Home Security: "Experience shows that effective arrangements for dealing with animal casualties and for caring for the domestic pets of homeless people plays an important part in the maintaining of public morale after air raids."

  Footnote Nina was the wife of the thirteenth Duke of Hamilton who died on 16 March 1940. Three of their four sons – Lord Douglas Douglas-Hamilton, Lord C.N. Douglas-Hamilton and Lord Malcolm Douglas-Hamilton were serving with the RAF at the outbreak of war. The first he fourteenth Duke, had been chief pilot of the Mount Everest flight expedition in 1933. Ferne Animal Sanctuary survives, but is now at Wambrook, Somerset.

1 November   **Rail-guns brought to Purbeck.**

Two 12-inch Mark 11 railway mounted howitzers are now in the Isle of Purbeck where the first gun-spur has been made ready near Furzebrook by the 14th Super Heavy Battery of 5th Corps the Royal Artillery. The gunners came down from Catterick, Yorkshire, on 15 October and have now been united with their weapons.

  The guns are being pulled by a Drummond K10 class mixed traffic locomotive, a 4-4-0, number 393.

1 November   **Anti-Aircraft Co-operation Unit at Christchurch.**

H-Flight of the No.1 Anti-Aircraft Co-operation Unit has arrived at Christchurch Aerodrome from Gosport. Its varied assortment of the older types of aeroplane, including Avro Ansons, Tiger Moths, a Fairey Battle, Miles Magister and a Bristol Blenheim, will be at the disposal of research scientists, who are working on countermeasures against the German bombers, at the Air Defence Experimental Establishment at Christchurch.

  Footnote The trials, which also involved Westland Lysanders, lasted until the end of July 1941.

3 November   **Motor-cycles leave Blandford.**

The Blandford Camp Reconnaissance Battalion, the 4th Battalion of the Royal Northumberland Fusiliers, are leaving Dorset today for Amesbury Abbey, Wiltshire.

6 November   **Heinkel lands at Bridport — thinking it is France.**

In the early morning a Heinkel 111 of Kampfgruppe 100, the elite two per cent of German bombers operating from Vannes, Brittany, and acting as pathfinders for the attacking formations, suffered a compass failure. It was confused by the British masking of German radio beacons into thinking it was back over France when in fact it was running out of fuel above Dorset.

The pilot landed on the shingle beach at West Bay, Bridport, and three out of the four crew survived – though they soon had their illusions shattered regarding France and found themselves in captivity. Soldiers guarded the aircraft, which carries the identification code "6N", and had some difference of opinion with a naval detachment that came to drag the plane up the beach. The soldiers followed orders not to let anyone touch the bomber and it was engulfed by the tide.

The aircraft has three vertical aerials and related radio equipment. This apparatus is to be salvaged for inspection by the Air Ministry boffins.

November   **Both rail-guns now operational in Purbeck.**

Another gun-spur has been completed at Furzebrook, on the heath north-west of Corfe Castle, for the second railway mounted 12-inch howitzer. It is positioned three hundred yards from the gun that was emplaced on 1 November — but this time after some difficulty as it was brought down the branch line facing the wrong way.

Last night the gun had to be taken to Swanage to go round the turntable there so that it now points towards the coast. Both guns can fire 750-lb. of high explosives at three minute intervals and are controlled by observation posts on Ballard Down to the east, East Man to the south-east and Tyneham Cap to the south-west.

They have a range of eight miles and are targeted on prospective invasion beaches. To protect them from air attack they have been draped With 4,200 yards of Cullacort netting, suspended between the pines on 3,456-feet of scaffolding and 10,400-yards of wire.

14 November   **Junkers explodes on a Poole cobbler's shed.**

This morning No. 10 Group Fighter Command, at its headquarters near Bath, plotted a single German reconnaissance aircraft crossing into the Middle Wallop sector from France. Pilot Officer Eric "Boy" Marrs, flying Spitfire R6968 with 152 Squadron, and Sergeant Pilot Albert Wallace "Bill" Kearsey, in Spitfire P9427, were scrambled from Warmwell to investigate.

Kearsey spotted the intruder, on a course for Yeovil or Bristol, between Blandford and Sturminster Newton. Both Spitfires attacked and the Junkers Ju88 turned for the Channel. The German was at 24,000 feet.

Marrs engaged it first, coming up from underneath to 150-yards and giving a burst that "started a fire under the port engine, an ominous red glow being clearly visible". Not that Marrs could take any further part in the action: "Unfortunately the rear gunner of the Junkers 88 landed one plumb in the middle of my windscreen, splintering it in all directions and making it quite opaque."

Kearsey was still "going hard at it" and the Ju88 dropped to 5,000 feet. The Warmwell pilots caught up with it over Poole where the smoking German aircraft, via its determined rear gunner and the pilot's last struggle with the controls, desperately attempted to effect a different ending.

Marrs had withdrawn, forced to become an observer by his shattered windscreen, and Kearsey found himself out of ammunition. By this time the Junkers was becoming a fireball. One of the four crewmen dropped out but his parachute failed to open and his body fell through the roof of Kinson Potteries.

The pilot, Oberleutnant A. von Kugelgen, may have been making some last attempt to level the plane but it hit the ground near the corner of Ringwood Road and Herbert Avenue, exploding fifty feet from a cobbler's shed. Mr Stainer and his family had narrow escapes, as did their neighbours. One night-time fire watcher was trapped in his bed by roof debris. Part of the fuselage ended up in the roof of Moore's Garage.

15 November Coventry bombers pass over Christchurch.

Last night a massed formation of some 150 German planes flew across the channel on a directional radio beam from the Cherbourg peninsula and crossed the coast at Christchurch and New Milton. They then headed up the Avon valley and passed two miles to the east of Salisbury.

Their code name for the operation was "Moonlight Sonata" and they were one of three streams of German aeroplanes — totalling 449 aircraft — aiming for Target 53, which turned out to be Coventry.

The other streams crossed the English coast over Dover and the Wash.

The landmark of Coventry Cathedral would be targeted by the pathfinders of Kampfgruppe 100. The city was devastated by 1,500 bombs [503-tons] leaving 568 dead and many more injured, and the cathedral and a third of the factories destroyed. The total number of damaged houses is estimated at 60,000. Only one German bomber was lost, over Loughborough.

15 November Escape flight from Belgium to Dorchester.

Two officers have escaped from Belgium in a light aeroplane which they took from an air-field near Dinant. They flew down the English Channel and landed in the Dorset countryside near Dorchester. One of the men is Belgian and the other French.

16 November Four killed in Poole blast.

Sidney Sherwood and his sons, Fred, Henry and Robert, were killed when a parachute mine landed on their home in Fancy Road, Poole, early this morning.

There were other blasts in Haskell's Road and Cynthia Road, causing serious injuries. Though she was able to protect her daughter, Molly, Mrs Lilian Kitkat was badly lacerated by flying debris and lost an eye.

16 November   **Fifty-three died in Bournemouth raid.**

German bombers attacked Bournemouth last night and left major destruction in three suburbs. At about 03.30 hours today six parachute mines floated down on Westbourne, Malmesbury Park Road, St Leonards Road, Turbary Common and Alma Road Schools. High explosive bombs and incendiaries have fallen at Gervis Road East, Meyrick Road, Knyveton Road, Groveley Manor, Terrace Road, Leven Avenue, Montague Road and Southern Avenue. Fifty-three people have been killed and 2,321 properties damaged.

Footnote   This was by far the worst of Bournemouth's five November raids. In total that month, in addition to the six parachute mines, the town received a total of twenty-four high explosive bombs and a number of incendiary devices. Sixty-two people were killed, 132 injured and 2,829 properties damaged.

16 November   **R.L. Stevenson's house is bombed.**

Last night's Bournemouth air-raid badly damaged Skerryvore, Robert Louis Stevenson's home at Westbourne — near the head of Alum Chine — where he lived from 1885 until he left for the Pacific in 1887. Two poems about the house appeared that year in *Underwood*.

Footnote   Pleas for it's restoration were ignored and the remains of the house were demolished in 1941. In 1954 the site became a municipal garden, with the footings of the house marked in concrete and a model erected of the Skerryvore lighthouse. Perhaps it would have been saved if he had written *Treasure Island* there; probably not. *Kidnapped* and *The Strange Case of Dr Jekyll and Mr Hyde* were written while he was living in Bournemouth.

17 November   **Parachute mine devastates Chapelhay, Weymouth.**

At 21.00 hours, when the Jack Buchanan programme had finished on the wireless, a German raider glided over Weymouth — he is said to have cut his engine — and dropped a parachute mine.

This caused the town's worst explosion of the war, destroying seventy-seven of the tightly packed terraced houses at Chapelhay and inflicting damage on another 879 properties. Twelve died, including children.

The device had been intended for the harbour – investigation of its remnants showed it was a sea mine.

18 November   **Poole houses evacuated.**

Houses in Newtown, at Poole, were evacuated last night after an unexploded bomb had created a large crater in Gwynne Road. Not that it was anything like as large as the hole left by the bomb that did explode in Grove Road — you could put a house in that one!

21 November   **West Bay bomber could have foiled Coventry raid.**

Scientists at the Royal Aircraft Establishment, Farnborough, have reassembled radio beam-flying equipment removed from the Heinkel He111 bomber of the Luftwaffe's pathfinding Kampfgruppe 100 which crash-landed at West Bay on 6 November. The aircraft had three vertical aerials and an intact X-Gerät radio receiver, also known as Wotan I, which is used for precision bombing by enabling the aircraft to follow a radio direction beam emanating from the Cherbourg peninsula.

What has surprised the Air Ministry boffins is that the apparatus is tuned to 2000 cycles per second (approximating to the "C" which is two octaves above standard-pitch middle "C"), whereas British jamming countermeasures had assumed a note of 1500 cycles (approximating to the "G" below this upper "C").

They are less than pleased that the vital equipment was corroded and full of sand, this avoidable damage to the delicate light alloy components being due to the crass folly of the Dorset soldiers who prevented sailors from pulling the aircraft up the beach to safety. It became awash with the rising tide.

Particular anger has been expressed that the secret could have been cracked in time to foil the Coventry raid, which took place a week ago: "Someone in Dorset should be shot!"

Footnote The significance of the discovery, and the frustrations it unleashed, are outlined by Dr Reg Jones, who was head of scientific intelligence at the Air Ministry, in his *Most Secret War*:

"So the filter could distinguish between the true beam and our jamming, even though we had got the radio frequencies correct. It was one of those instances where enormous trouble is taken to get the difficult parts right and then a slip-up occurs because of the lack of attention to a seemingly trivial detail."

This revelation came too late to prevent the Coventry raid but it did ensure that radio countermeasures were perfected by the Telecommunications Research Establishment in time to save the vital Rolls-Royce aero engine plant at Derby. On the night of 8 May 1941, in moonlit conditions similar to those of the Coventry raid, Derby's bombs fell on Nottingham – and those intended for Nottingham fell into open fields.

27 November   **Spitfire follows a Junkers to France.**

Though denied permission to intercept a Junkers Ju88 that was heading south-west from Southampton, Flight Lieutenant John Dundas was allowed to take up his section of 609 Squadron on a "practice flight" instead. The two Spitfires climbed rapidly and found the German bomber at 22,000 feet over Poole Bay, flying into the sun. Throttling to 2,600 revolutions the fighters' Merlin engines gave 280 miles per hour as the Spitfires closed on their target in its descent towards the Cherbourg peninsula. Dundas put Spitfire X4586 into an attacking glide at 14,000 feet, firing with five-second bursts at 400, 300 and then 200 yards.

Flames shot out of the Ju88's port engine and it lurched out of control as they crossed the French coast. There being a German aerodrome below, the Spitfires did not follow their quarry any further towards the ground, but turned north-west for the eighty mile return flight to RAF Warmwell.

28 November   **609 Squadron loses two for a Luftwaffe ace.**

"I've finished an Me109 – whoopee!" These were the last words received by radio from Flight Lieutenant John Dundas, flying Spitfire X4586 with 609 Squadron from RAF Warmwell.

Dundas had scrambled at 15.50 hours. Missing also is Pilot Officer P.A. Baillon in Spitfire R6631. Both were over the sea off the Isle of Wight.

Tonight German radio announced that the Luftwaffe had lost one of its ace fighter pilots, Major Helmut Wick, who had 57 white kill-bars painted on the rudder of his Messerschmitt Bf109E. He was leading Jagdgeschwader 2.

28 November   **Warmwell's 152 Squadron also loses two Spitfires.**

Having congratulated itself on an "unusually quiet most of November" the month has been marred for 152 Squadron at Warmwell Aerodrome by the loss of two pilots today.

Polish Sergeant Pilot Zygmunt Klein's Spitfire, P9427, fell into the sea and Pilot Officer Arthur Ray Watson, flying Spitfire R6597, crashed near Wareham, as a result of dog-fights with Bf109s over Poole Bay and off the Needles, Isle of Wight.

The Polish sergeant "just disappeared" but Watson "bungled his baling out and tore his parachute" which "streamed out behind him but owing to the tears did not open".

Watson's death was avenged almost immediately by Pilot Officer Eric "Boy" Marrs in Spitfire R6968. He crept up slowly on the culprit Bf109, staying in his blindest spot, until he was within a hundred yards.

Marrs fired for just a second, unleashing 55 rounds of .303 ammunition from each of his eight guns – "the easiest victory I've had". There was an instant result:

"Black smoke belched forth and oil spattered over my windscreen. He half rolled and dived away. I followed in a steep spiral to see what was going to happen but my speed became so great I pulled away and my wing hid him for a bit.

"When I looked again there was a large number of flaming fragments waffling down to the sea. One large black lump, which was not on fire, trailed a white plume which snapped open and became a parachute. This was the pilot, and he must have baled out just before the petrol tank blew up. However, he landed in the sea and might just as well have blown up, for he was never found."

29 November   **Spitfire plunges into Field Grove, near Durweston.**

15.14 hours. A flight from 152 Squadron, including Spitfire R6907 flown by Pilot Officer John Woodward Allen, was scrambled because of a suspected enemy fighter sweep. They were instructed to patrol a circuit of RAF Warmwell at 25,000 feet.

Allen sent a radio message but it was unintelligible and nothing further was heard from him. His Spitfire was then seen to break away and dive shallowly, though under control. Suddenly it plummeted vertically into the ground and completely disintegrated on impact. The severity of the crash precluded any mechanical examination. It is thought the pilot fainted because of loss of oxygen. He had been flying Spitfires for three weeks. The fighter crashed at Field Grove, a wood half a mile west of Travellers' Rest, on the downs two miles south-west of Durweston.

Footnote The crash site was marked by a plaque, replaced in 1978 by a granite memorial.

Ernest Day of Okeford Fitzpaine recalled seeing the plane in difficulties: "It was late afternoon, the day that a sixpence fell from the sky, hit my right shoulder and fell in the main road at Thornicombe. The fighter was climbing. Then I saw, very high in the sky, three German bombers returning from Bristol. The fighter made one attack on the bombers, then slowly descended towards me for a while, then it came straight down towards the ground with the throttle open.

"I stood thinking it was going straight into the ground, nose first, about fifty yards from me. Then what seemed like seconds before hitting the ground the throttle closed and the fighter turned out of the dive very sharply, just missing the ground by inches.

"It proceeded on a course towards Blandford, very unsteadily, just missing the telegraph poles on Thornicombe Hill, but slowly gaining height. When it reached Gipsy's Corner it turned left, then it flew over Fairmile where it slowly descended and went out of my view. A few hours later a friend told me that the fighter crashed near Travellers' Rest."

30 November   **Bf109 belly-lands on Purbeck spy mission.**

Unteroffizier Paul Wacker of JG 27, who was flying a Messerschmitt Bf109 fighter-bomber belonging to Staffel 4 of Lehrgeschwader 2 – a unit testing improvised aircraft under operational conditions – suffered engine failure whilst on a weather reconnaissance over Swanage this afternoon. He was fortunate to belly-land on fields at Woodyhyde Farm, beside the railway between Swanage and Corfe Castle, narrowly avoiding heavily wooded countryside.

Footnote The tail section of his machine survives. It was used to repair the captured test-flown Bf109 that is now in the Royal Air Force Museum at Hendon.

1 December   **Bournemouth AA gunners claim two planes.**

This evening and last night there was bombing at Southampton and the enemy aircraft were harassed by Hurricanes and anti-aircraft fire as they flew over Poole Bay and Bournemouth.

Six German aircraft were shot down — two of them being claimed by anti-aircraft gunners. One of the planes dropped into the sea off Hengistbury Head.

2 December   **Warmwell's Europeans claim double kill.**

The flying partnership of 609 Squadron's two eastern Europeans, Pilot Officers Noel le Chevalier Agazarian and Tadeusz Nowierski, today achieved a double kill.

Scrambled from RAF Warmwell, they intercepted German aircraft off Thorney Island, Hampshire, and shared the destruction of a Messerschmitt Bf110 fighter-bomber and a Dornier Do17 bomber. The Spitfires broke up an attacking formation that was heading for Portsmouth.

Footnote Agazarian was then posted to the Middle East and lost his life when 274 Squadron was intercepted by Messerschmitt Bf109s over the Western Desert on 16 May 1941. He is buried in Knightsbridge War Cemetery at Acroma, Libya.

Nowierski became Polish Liaison Officer to Headquarters, 11 Group Fighter Command, in 1942, and would be promoted to Group Captain, commanding RAF Dunholme Lodge. He returned to Poland in 1947, and died in 1983.

3 December   **Hurn Aerodrome bombed.**

The aerodrome being built at Hurn, to the north of Bournemouth, had its first raid today. Five high explosive bombs and a number of incendiaries fell at 18.50 hours.

Footnote The site had previously been recommended by Sir Alan Cobham to Bournemouth Corporation for a municipal aerodrome, but in the event — a war — it was the Air Ministry that took the initiative, on behalf of the Royal Air Force.

Bournemouth's previous airfield, Ensbury Park Aerodrome and Racecourse, became a housing estate in 1932. Its first scheduled commercial flight, in a Handley Page bomber, was flown by William Sholto Douglas in 1919. By 1940 he would be Deputy Chief of the Air Staff, then Air Officer Commanding-in-Chief of Fighter Command in the midst of the conflicts of 1940-42, finishing the war as Marshal of the Royal Air Force and retiring in 1948 as first Baron Douglas of Kirtleside.

13 December   **Christchurch families evacuated just in time.**

Families between Freda Road and Kings Avenue, Christchurch, were evacuated from their homes just in time this evening. A crater with an unexploded bomb, outside 1 Kings Avenue, had been reported at 09.25 hours but the decision to clear the area was not taken until 17.25. A bomb disposal team had then taken a look and decided to leave the bomb for 96 hours.

At 18.55, however, it went off – damaging three houses and rupturing gas and water pipes.

20 December   **Alexander and Montgomery see Studland Bay set ablaze.**

General Harold Alexander, General Officer Commanding-in-Chief of Southern Command, and Major-General Bernard Montgomery of 5th Corps, today stood on the clifftop between Redend Point and Old Harry Rocks, Studland, to watch the sea on fire. Pipes have been laid from the beach in Project Fougasse to release oil in a series of slicks to form a continuous strip that is then ignited. It has been a calm day and the water was burning; waves would disperse the slick, though on the other hand the enemy is likely to choose a day when landing conditions are favourable.

Footnote The intention had been to repeat the exercise in the night, because British intelligence suggested that the German troops feared a conflagration on the beaches, but this was a disappointment due to waves lashed up by a cold on-shore wind.

24 December   **E-boats sink two ships off Dorset.**

Convoy FN 366, sailing between Portland and the Isle of Wight, was last night attacked by the German 1st Schnellboot Flotilla (of six E-boats, S26, S28, S29, S34, S56 and S59). The enemy torpedo boats sank a Dutch ship, the *Maastricht*, and a Royal Navy armed trawler, HMT *Pelton*.

25 December   **Mobile radar goes into the field at Sopley.**

A mobile ground-to-air radar antenna, developed by the Telecommunications Research Establishment at Worth Matravers and built at Somerford, Christchurch, by the Air Defence Experimental Establishment, is being tested for the first time today in the countryside. Known as Type 15 the unit has been placed on a flat part of Lord Manners's estate at Sopley, between the River Avon and the New Forest.

December   **Blandford's Battle Training Camp.**

Blandford Camp is now designated a Battle Training Camp and provides a variety of intensive assault courses to simulate combat conditions.

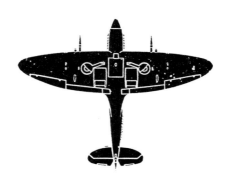

Index